INVITING DESIRE

A guide for women who want to enhance their sex life

WALKER J. THORNTON

Published in the United States by Silver Spiral Press
P.O. Box 8341
Charlottesville, VA 22906
www.silverspiralpress.com

Author Photo @Constance & Eric, 2015,
www.constance&eric.com
Cover Design by Sarah Crossland
Cover image by alla_snesar, iStock
Logo design by Julia Parlette-Cariño

ISBN: 0-9976019-0-9
ISBN-13: 978-0-9976019-0-9

For Dave, your support, encouragement, and willingness to explore and participate in my personal journey made it all possible.

CONTENTS

ACKNOWLEDGMENTS

I want to offer a big thank you to the many women who provided the inspiration to write this book. Your questions and comments and cheerleading gave me the courage to keep doing what I do.

Thanks to Jeff Coomer for his friendship, his nudging, and thoughtful observations on the writing and publishing process. I couldn't have done it without my Developmental Editor, Dvora Konstant, of Dvorak Ink, for her insight and useful suggestions, along with much needed editing. And to the friends who listened and offered feedback during my writing process, especially Sue Fogg.

If sexuality is one dimension of our ability to live passionately in the world then in cutting off our sexual feelings we diminish our overall power to feel, know and value deeply.

— Judith Plaskow (1)

WALKER THORNTON

INTRODUCTION

Inviting Desire is about awakenings, sexual and otherwise. This book offers you a series of approaches—writings, images, exercises, and other resources—to deepen your awareness of your body and senses and learn how to embrace yourself as a sexual individual.

It is a book about self-love and self-respect. It is about finding enjoyment in your body—physically and emotionally. *Inviting Desire* is not about reversing the aging process, dieting, or getting a new makeup regime. No need to 'reinvent' yourself or contemplate plastic surgery to become more in touch with your sexuality—you already have the necessary ingredients—a rich map of your abundant life of gifts and talents. We will explore and discover those as we begin this journey together.

You, My Reader

I am a heterosexual woman, so I tend to write from that perspective, referring to traditional male-female relationships, but I believe this book will work for any person who identifies as a woman and who seeks sexual pleasure, regardless of whom the partner is. The word 'partner' can be a husband, wife, lover(s), friend with benefits—whomever it applies to in your life. In some cases the material is very clearly talking about heterosexual sex.

Some of you are not currently in relationships. This book is for you as well. Our sexuality, the quest for pleasure, does not disappear if we are single.

Women in their menopausal years often speak to me of losing their desire or feeling less interest in sex—you are my main audience. Yet, women of all ages and stages of life have times when their sexual feelings shift or demand a little more attention. We are always learning and always seeking ways to have pleasurable moments in our lives.

The premise of this book is that you must, and can, take ownership of your own sexual desire. It starts with you—your thought processes, your senses, and your ability and desire to connect with your body. Where you go with this new sense of yourself as a sexual being depends on your life, your goals, and your relationship status.

Inviting Desire is just for you. It is *not* for you and a partner. It is *not* for your partner, though I imagine a partner could benefit from reading or discussing the book with you. This is about you, your body, and your desire. In a society where men are viewed as the initiators and 'owners' of sex, women are not encouraged to own their sexuality. Using this book as your guide, you will learn to take ownership of your sexuality.

4

Desire originates in your mind, in your body—so it's important for you to view this process of awakening your body as all about you. For that reason, there is not a lot of content focused on partnered sex—we are talking about you and what you want for your body—how you choose to go about exploring relationships is in some ways secondary to the process.

But first, a word of caution. This book is not designed to fix a broken relationship, solve communication problems, or bring a desired partner into your life. If you are experiencing physical or health-related issues, please see your healthcare practitioner. If you have a partner, they will have to adjust to this new you and that can be scary—for both of you. Risk is always present when we open ourselves up to growth and change. Ah, but the possible rewards! What this book will do is assist you in exploring and deepening your sexual desires. Comfort with your body will lead to greater satisfaction with your life and a deeper appreciation of what you offer the world.

My Story

In 2000 I informed my husband of 24 years that I wanted a divorce. At that point my desire, libido, was buried under years of stress, discontent, and all the garbage I had failed to address in my life. I began dating shortly afterwards, thinking I was desperate for sex after almost 2 years of no sex, but what I was really looking for was a mixture of companionship and intimacy—neither of which I was ready for at that point in time. The sexual me had shut down in the last years of my marriage. And the neediness I presented to men was often disastrous. It took me several years of awkward dating, bad sex, frustration, and loneliness to figure out that something needed to change. I began working with a therapist and I began to blog, anonymously, about my dating escapades.

I started putting myself first and becoming a little more intentional about the men I chose to date. I still made plenty of mistakes.

In 2010 I quit my job and found myself, a single woman in her mid-50's, without employment. My life-long love of writing became the vehicle for my next job. I began writing professionally, moving from blogging to writing openly about sex, dating, and relationships in midlife and beyond. Using my skills as a speaker and educator, and my experience in the field of violence against women, I begin speaking at sexuality conferences and to smaller audiences about midlife women and sexuality.

In the process of writing for various websites about midlife women and sex, women began reaching out to me with their concerns. The common thread in their questions and stories was the challenge of navigating sex and relationships as they aged—often without resources tailored to the needs of older women. As I studied sexuality and began to interact with other sex educators, I was having my own sexual exploration. The interest in my work spilled over to my sex life and I began to open up in new ways. A willing and eager lover was more than happy to learn and explore with me. He never said no to anything I suggested. Exploring sexuality in that loving and safe environment helped to inform my work and brought me to this place.

As I write this, I am 61. And, I'm having the best sex of my life—I have learned how to ask for what I need (most of the time) and to create experiences that bring me pleasure. I no longer have sex just to please a man. I have sex on my terms and find enjoyment there. Where once finding desire was challenging I now know how to create the environment I want. I have a higher level of arousal and desire than I did in my 20's and 30's.

Whether you're single, divorced, widowed, in an unfulfilling relationship or marriage or simply want to expand your capacity for pleasure, this book is designed to help you find your way to pleasure. You might be happily partnered but yearn to experience more—this book is for you, too.

What To Expect When Reading This Book

I suggest you read the book from front to back, following the recommended daily path, as the exercises build on each other. The book is written as a 30-day journey but you may want to spend more time on certain days. Take your time. If you are one of those curious people who want to jump around—please do, you'll find something to engage you on every page.

The book is loosely divided into sections. We start by getting to know more about the body and the senses, and how to take care of yourself. From there I walk you through what I think of as the essentials for a sexy life—a sort of "sexy toolkit." As you get a better understanding of your own capacity for desire, we explore communicating wants and needs with partners and finally, how to continue to invite desire into your life after you finish reading the book.

What You Will Need As You Begin This Journey

As we spend the next 30 days together there are a few things you will need. First is a willing and open attitude. This book may ask you to stretch a little, to allow yourself to get uncomfortable. But I believe that the rewards are many—and you are here because you want to regain that "old" desire. You want to feel alive. You want a juicer sex life. You can modify the exercises to fit your needs, but I do encourage you to take the time to go through the daily exercise. They don't all require a lot of time and will help you process what you're learning and articulate your wants and needs. Think of it as an investment in you.

Select a notebook or journal for this series. I ask you to record thoughts, inspirations, and ideas, which you will revisit over the course of reading the book and in the future. Your first sensuous exercise can be in the choosing of your notebook. Select one that appeals to you–whether it's the color, the design or the feel of the paper—make it something you'll enjoy picking up every day.

By reading this book, you've agreed to engage your sexuality. It's one of the most powerful acts of self-care you can engage in. It is a gift you give yourself. Thank you for seeing yourself as worthy of this journey. And thank you for trusting me to be a part of your journey.

DAY 1

TOUCH

The minute you start reveling in the textures of life and the world of the senses, you find yourself thinking about love.

-Diane Ackerman, *A Natural History of Love (1)*

It's often said that the mind is a woman's primary sex organ. To gain the greatest pleasure we must be open, receptive, and desirous of pleasure. For many of us this means we have to engage our brains in sensuous thoughts.

One of the best ways to do that is through paying attention to the senses. Our senses allow us to experience our selves and our environment, leading to a heightened awareness. As a result we become more attuned to pleasure.

How often do you literally stop to smell the flowers, to touch the objects around you, to listen or taste? These first days are a bit like the practice of mindfulness. We are going to start by looking at the sense of touch.

As you go through your day try touching your surroundings.

- What does it feel like to run your hands across a polished wood surface or the cool smooth hardness of your kitchen counter?
- What about a satiny nightgown or slip? Feel the way it slides across your body. Feel the silky softness as it caresses your body.

Start by focusing on your hands:

- Do you caress with fingertips or an open palm? Try stroking your hand, running down from fingertips to palm. What does it feel like? Ticklish, prickly? Does your skin tingle? Are your hands smooth or rough? Does one hand have more sensation than the other?
- Imagine a lover touching you. What kind of strokes would you like that person to use?
- When you bathe, use your hands instead of the washcloth. Enjoy the soapy, gliding sensation of skin touching skin. Do you prefer the gentle sensation of your hand washing your body or the rougher texture of a washcloth? How does your skin feel as the drops of water beat against you? Turn the stream of water so it's focused on one part of your body and feel the water as it hits your skin. Is it too hard or stimulating?

Focus on the sensations. Allow yourself to linger in the moment. *Imagine your skin awakening.*

Awakening our bodies is the first step to experiencing greater pleasure. It's easy to get caught up in our daily routines and forget to physically engage with our surroundings. If we practice creating pleasurable sensations for our bodies, we may crave more. We begin to learn what kind of touch pleases and awakens us.

Daily Exercise:

- As you go through your day, write down the things you enjoy touching or feeling against your skin. Note the sensations, pleasant and uncomfortable. Try to capture these thoughts as they occur. Writing or talking about the sensations and feelings you experience helps the brain connect feeling with thought.
- Create a list of desired touches, or physical sensations. They might include a feather gently caressing your body, running your hands through freshly mown grass, bare feet in an outdoor fountain or stream, soft puppy fur.

What does your skin desire?

DAY 2

TASTE

Food has always held sex appeal. Historically, certain foods like chocolate, strawberries, champagne, and oysters were thought to act as aphrodisiacs, increasing sexual desire. Food and drink can come to be associated with sensuous moments. The most basic foods come alive when you eat them for enjoyment or when shared with a loved one.

Think about foods you enjoy, or that have a sensuous quality. Imagine eating crème brulee or a dark chocolate mousse. Maybe you prefer a ripe blue cheese or a melt-in-your-mouth steak?

Savor your food, feel the textures of the food, the sensation on your tongue. Imagine a ripe fruit, the juices exploding in your mouth, or the creaminess of a certain food, prepared to perfection.

Eating slowly and indulging in the pleasurable sensation of the food is what turns a meal into a sensuous experience.

What do you crave? Do you want to run your finger across your plate and lick the chocolate from your fingers? Or taste the spiciness on your lover's lips? Do you want to drizzle him with honey and lick it off?

As we awaken all of our senses, we look to food not just as fuel for our bodies but as something to excite and awaken our sense of taste and smell. In talking about the ways to awaken our desires, we will include all aspects of pleasure—not just the "expected" sexual ones.

Being "turned on" starts with the mind. We can find all kinds of pairings to awaken and inspire us. Think about foods you've had in the past that were so exquisite your body responded positively.

Imagine the textures on your tongue, the aromas and smells. Spicy curries served with cool cucumber sauce. A tart raspberry sauce drizzled on rich chocolate cake, eaten slowly while savoring the combination of flavors and textures.

Now imagine a lover sharing those foods with you. Food can nourish more than physical hunger. As you begin to think about how food feeds your senses and your desires you can begin to understand the sensuous appeal of foods.

Check out these movies with sexy food themes: *9½ Weeks, Like Water for Chocolate,* and *Chocolat.*

Daily Exercise:

- Plan a special meal. It can be a cheese selection or a 4-course dinner. The key is to include foods that appeal to you. Think about the colors on your plate, paired with the right beverage, and table setting for your meal. What foods do you crave? Give yourself permission to indulge. Need ideas? Go to a specialty store and wander through the aisles sampling foods you've never tried. What looks appealing to you?

- Now think about creating that meal to share with a loved one. Will it be an outdoor picnic with cheeses, fruits, and wine? Maybe you prefer a candlelight dinner at your favorite restaurant.

What about a tray of little dishes to share in bed—
imagine feeding each other, sensuous play
wrapped up in the act of tasting. Imagine the
possibilities for creating a sexy moment with food,
even if you're alone.

DAY 3

WORDS

I have hunger for your mouth, for your voice, for your hair
And through streets I go not nourishing myself, quiet,
Bread does not sustain me, the dawn drives me mad,
I look for the liquid sound of your feet in the day.

I am hungry for your laugh that slips,
for your hands the colour of a furious harvest,
I have hunger for the pale stones of your fingernails,
I want to eat your skin like an untouched almond

I want to eat the sunbeam burnt in your beauty,
the sovereign nose of the arrogant face,
I want to eat the fleeting shadow of your lashes

and hungry I come and go sniffing the twilight
looking for you, looking for your hot heart
like a puma in the solitude of Quitratue.

-Pablo Neruda, 100 Love Sonnets

Words have such power. We are easily seduced by them, persuaded, cajoled, and aroused.

To explore words is to experience their sensuous qualities. Think about a time when a description you heard, or read, was so vivid that you found yourself transported. Words tie us to our other senses. They evoke an emotional response—sadness, anger, happiness, feeling sexy...

Let's consider erotica. Are you turned on by reading sexy stories? I'll never forget the powerful impression D.H. Lawrence's *Lady Chatterley's Lover* made on me in my late teens.

What if reading a sexy book kindled your desire, making you want sex?

A book doesn't have to be sexually explicit in order to stimulate desire. There are many books in the romance genre with erotic content. Here are a few suggestions that you might enjoy.

- The poetry of Pablo Neruda –Reviewers have called this Chilean poet "a frank, sensuous spokesman for love." *(1)*
- *Lady Chatterley's Lover* by D.H. Lawrence – An infamous novel about a lonely wife and her lover, written in 1928. *(2)*
- *My Secret Garden:* by Nancy Friday–A classic collection of stories about ordinary women and their private fantasies. *(3)*
- *Free Fall, A Late-in-Life Love Affair* by Rae Padilla Francoeur – A 55-year-old woman finds a new love affair, and celebrating her sexuality, rediscovers herself. *(4)*
- The writings of Anaïs Nin, a French writer of erotica, memoir, and essays, with her first works

written in the 1930s. Many critics consider her one of the finest writers of female erotica. *(5)*

Treat yourself to a good book. Read it for your own pleasure or read it aloud with a partner. The idea is to explore your response to the written word.

Daily Exercise:

Pick up a sexy book or select some erotica on the internet. Consider the following questions.

- Does the idea of reading about sex excite you?
- Do you prefer suggestive or explicit language?
- Do you get ideas from reading sexy scenes?

If you enjoy erotica, you might begin to use it as a way of getting in the mood. On Day 7 we'll talk about ways you can use words, your own, your partner's, or erotic literature, to add some sizzle to your relationships.

DAY 4

VISUALIZE YOURSELF AS A SEXUAL BEING

The first 3 days of *Inviting Desire* focused on the senses–touch, taste, sound. As you begin to think, feel, and envision yourself as a woman who enjoys sensual pleasures, you may find yourself becoming more sexually awakened.

Now it's time to begin exploring your sexual desires, to make a playdate with pleasure. The goal of this book is to help you embrace your sexuality, to get to know your body, and how it responds to touch and other pleasures. I can offer you tools for your journey, but it's up to you to create the sexy life you want. You took the first step in buying this book! Part of the process of inviting desire into your life is imagining yourself as the sexual person you want to become.

Imagery, or visualizing, is powerful. It's akin to a rehearsal in some ways. Athletes are sometimes taught to visualize themselves crossing the finish line or making the shot. When we can *see* ourselves doing what we want, we are more likely to *do* it.

Awakening your sexual desire requires a similar process. The first step in the process is to see yourself as a sexual individual. That might mean forgetting everything you've been told about what 'sexy' looks like. Ignore the little voice that says you don't deserve it or that feeling good about yourself is selfish. Ignore the cultural message that older women no longer want or have sex. By creating our own imagery we set the tone and shape our "reality."

You want to create a sense of longing–for the touch of another person, the desire of skin on skin, the delicate play of lips and tongue. To think or read about it and feel a stirring deep inside. To forget about the unfinished chores, the job deadline, and allow your mind and body to be fully present to touch, yours or that of a lover.

Daily Exercise:

Over the next couple of days devote some time to daydreaming or fantasizing. Visualize yourself in an intimate moment. Imagine being in full-blown arousal. What would that look like?

- Can you imagine, or actually feel, the signs of arousal in your body–the tingle in your genitals, your nipples getting hard? Look at that appealing guy across the room; imagine brushing against him as you pass his chair. What would his lips feel like on the back of your neck? What would you like to say to him? Try to imagine what it's like to feel sexually attracted to someone. It could be your current partner, Sharon Stone, or some random person you see on the street. Fantasize a little.
- Think about a relationship—current or soon-to-be—and what you would like to happen between the two of you. Write out the details of your desired sexual encounter. What will you wear? Will there be food or drink? Imagine the touch and kisses that will become part of your seduction. Plan it. Then allow yourself to indulge in the sensations.

- Are you flirty? Are you the type who might take a sip of your drink and, with wet lips, lean over and kiss your dinner date? Where do you touch him? A light caress on his hand? Running your fingers through his hair? Would you like to place your hand on his thigh? What gestures or words would you use to convey your growing desire? Do you lead or let him make the move? Are you brazen or demure? What excites you?

Take some time to think about how you might bring your fantasies to life. And have fun with it!

DAY 5

SELF-AFFIRMATION

And if I looked at myself in the mirror, I found myself flushed

and more beautiful at such moments. I felt like kissing my own

reflected image.

-George Sand (1)

Beauty is an internal thing. Each of us is beautiful, in a way that is uniquely our own. Our laugh, the way we hold our head, our gifts and talents—they define us and add dimension to who we are.

How do you feel about yourself today? If you're a woman in the throes of menopause the answer may fluctuate, along with your hormones, over the course of a day. When your body is out of sorts your life can feel a little chaotic as well. Menopause comes at the very time when we're going through other changes. Children may be leaving home, signs of aging are showing up subtly, and maybe things that worked in the past suddenly feel out of whack.

Thoughts of retirement, caring for aging parents, and the uncertainty of our world begin to weigh us down.

On those days you may not feel as beautiful or loveable.

How, in the midst of all this turmoil, do you make time to love yourself? Loving yourself requires a little effort. We often forget that. With so many demands for your attention, finding time to care for "me" is often the last thing on the to-do list.

On Day 6 we'll talk about pampering—a specific way of affirming your needs and placing the priority on you.

You are the most important person in your life. You have earned the right to pay attention to yourself. Here are some ideas on how to take care of yourself:

- Take 30 minutes, 4 hours, or a whole day off. Go on a playdate with yourself: go to a movie, take a nap, schedule a spa day, or spend the day in your PJs with a good book. Give yourself permission to let go, check out, and indulge.

- Speak out about what you need. Tell the boss you need an hour. Say "No" more often. Declare freedom from cooking dinner. Tell your partner where and how you like to be touched. Ask for what you want.

- Take inventory. List the things that you want to change in your life. Journaling is a great way to let it all out. Just start writing. You're not committing to anything, you're simply exploring unspoken thoughts—thoughts you didn't know existed.

- Unclutter a space in your house. Start with a 15-minute plan to eliminate things you don't need or want any more. Freeing up space can give you a mental boost as well.

- Turn off the cell phone, shut down the computer. Walk away from your technology. Everyone will wait—this is your time.

You will find that taking care of your needs is deeply

satisfying. This conscious act of affirming yourself is all about valuing *you*.

Why Is This Beneficial?

It's difficult to feel sexy if you feel tired or stressed or you don't feel valued—by yourself or others around you. The simple act of creating a little "me time" to step away and relax can do wonders for your emotional health. Your sexual energy is tied to how you feel about yourself and your surroundings.

Taking charge and creating your ideal environment creates literal and figurative space for you to expand.

Uncluttering, clearing your calendar, or letting go of what no longer serves you is about respecting your own needs. The process is one of setting priorities. *You* become the priority.

Daily Exercise:

- Get out your journal and write down the things that get you down. What's holding you back or making you feel a little stressed in your daily life? It can be a short list or you can dump all of those frustrations on paper.

- Once you've got a few written down, tackle one of the things on the list. It could be that you need to take a short walk or spend a few minutes straightening a cluttered spot in your house. Once you've completed that task take a few more minutes to sit down and give yourself permission to relax. Just be still and settle into that spot. Give yourself a little love. Say something affirming. Congratulate yourself. Do the same thing the next day until you've checked off most of the things on your list.

- Make a list of all the positive things in your life. It could be as simple as "I have great hair" to having gratitude for the energy gained after clearing that stack of old mail on your desk. I do this every night by naming at least one "Joy" for the day as I fall asleep. It might be about what someone has done for me. It might be the recognition of a simple pleasure. A day of sunshine or a friendly smile. It is a practice that reminds me to focus on the good.

DAY 6

PAMPERING

If the body is a temple how do you worship yours?

Pampering isn't necessarily something frivolous; it can be thought of as an act of self-care. Showing yourself love and respect is an ideal starting point if you want to open yourself up to better sex, to feeling more vibrant and sexual.

One of my favorite forms of self-care is to get a massage. I love the scented oils and the soothing touch of a massage therapist kneading and caressing my body. It's a sensuous experience that relaxes me and stimulates my senses.

Self-care is important for a couple of reasons. Reducing or eliminating stress and tension helps you feel more relaxed and contributes to an overall sense of well-being. It's difficult to feel sexy if you're feeling tired or stressed.

The act of indulging, or pampering yourself, is really about honoring yourself as someone worthy of being taken care of. It's a way of saying, "I care about myself." When you cultivate a sense of well-being and understand that self-care is acceptable, even desirable, you're more likely to feel interested in sex. When your body feels good you're more likely to feel comfortable in intimate moments, and in giving and receiving with a partner. If you don't think of yourself as worthy of that attention you're not likely to derive as much pleasure from intimate moments.

Maybe you were raised to believe your role as a woman meant you had to take care of others. If you are married and/or have children you probably felt their needs were more important than your own. Giving yourself permission to attend to your own needs is something most women have to practice.

The idea behind today's message is to treat yourself to something special. If you live alone or have no regular physical touch from another person, it's easy to become desensitized. Humans need touch. We need to experience connection and intimacy. Taking care of ourselves is a great way to start.

- Consider a manicure or pedicure—soaking, being massaged with nourishing oils, and having your nails attended to is both soothing and invigorating. Why not take the time to schedule one this week?
- You can make a sensuous ritual out of putting lotion on your arms, legs, feet, or your whole body.
- Buy scented bath oil or body wash to add to your bathing routine. If you take baths, place candles near the tub and make bath time an event. Turn off the phone. Add your favorite music and a glass of wine for a relaxing experience.

What rituals make you feel good? Think about the simple routines you practice and how they make you feel. If you don't have any routines—then it's time for you to start paying more attention to your needs.

Daily Exercise:

- Take a few minutes, with your eyes closed, to relax into your body and do a mental scan. Start at the top of your head and work your way down to the toes, "listening" to each part of your body. How is your body? Is it feeling content? Is it comfortable and relaxed or achy and stressed out? Jaws clenched or relaxed? Shoulders up and tight? Really feel what's going on. Feel the weight of your body in the chair, or bed.

- Our bodies talk to us; sometimes the message is subtle, sometimes it's shouting to get our attention. When we're tense or feeling down we can often feel it in a certain spot in our body. Try this little routine a couple of times a day—"listening"—as you begin to tune in to your body. You can touch yourself in the tight places to help them relax. Caress an achy elbow; rub your tummy in a loving way, relax your jaws. You are letting your body know it is being "heard" and taken care of.

- What self-care ritual would you like to add to your routine? What would make you feel relaxed and cared for? If you had a whole afternoon alone with the ability to have or do anything you wanted, what would it be? Make a plan and take one action right now to make that plan a reality. Make a reservation at the day spa, ask for a hug, plan lunch in the park, do something for yourself. For example, maybe you want new sheets for your bed, or a nice dinner at a new restaurant. Put it on your calendar. If you don't plan it now, when? This is about making *you* a priority.

DAY 7

THE POWER OF WORDS

We tend to think too narrowly about what sex actually is and it limits our imagination. What if we began to consider other forms of pleasure as sex? What happens when we pair activities with sexual desire? Desire begins in our minds, whether we're stimulated visually, tactilely, or by word, if we can associate those images with desire.

Words have real power for me so I want to share a story of how words can transform an encounter or a relationship into something deliciously sexy. You can use words and wordplay (defined by Merriam-Webster as a playful use of words)—shared or for your own private satisfaction—to help awaken your desire.

"We are drawn to each other because we understand the power of details." - M wrote to me.

He knows me well. He understands the power of words to seduce, arouse, tease, and put me into a state of suspension. Is it because we are both writers that this thread exists between us? It has been that way from the very first encounter, some 13 years ago, when he sent an erotic story as his initial communication and I responded that I was both turned on and turned off by his approach.

He would go on to write more erotic stories.

We found in each other the ability to transform the written word into a powerful tool. We seduce each other with words. Some days I have this fantasy of him writing on my body—a fine-pointed pen inscribing the words on my skin. In the hollow of my lower back as it curves upward to the rise of my cheeks. Words would circle my breasts, run across my belly button and disappear into pubic hair.

He possesses me with his words. They sink in and imprint themselves on me like magic. The ink seeping into my skin, my blood, and carrying our passion into every fiber of my being. That passion rules me. It owns me. He has that power over me; he knows it and uses it.

We often fail to explore all the avenues to awakening:
- The smell of his body as he comes near.
- The sensation of fingers running through my hair.
- The fresh linen-y smell of his starched shirt.
- Words, whispered, shouted, written on paper.

If we can associate those images (feel free to substitute your own) with desire, over time, the mere presence of the thoughts or words themselves begin to arouse our bodies. We build on them, we carry the words inside of us, we roll them across our tongue, and we feel their presence on and in our bodies.

What words would you use with a lover? You could pull from Pablo Neruda or Anais Nin, or you can develop your own. (See Day 3) The words don't have to be poetic. Start with sharing how you feel or what you want your lover to do.

- " I long to feel your lips on the nape of my neck…"
- "When you touch me, the sensation is like being on fire…"
- "Run your tongue along my breastbone."

Sometimes writing the words allow us to be more daring or playful than we might be face to face. My word lover and I play with the image of a silken thread. He speaks of wrapping me in the thinnest of red silk threads. I don't necessarily expect that to happen—the power is in imagining the experience.

Daily Exercise:

- The goal is to think differently about what holds sexual power for you. Using my story as an example, let's focus on words. (You do not have to be a writer to do this exercise.) If the idea of writing feels awkward, begin by describing an everyday event—taking a shower, brushing your teeth. What words can you use to add a sensuous note to what you're doing? Describe the sound of the water, the feeling of the drops on your skin. How does the soap smell? Are you rubbing slowly or using a rough cloth to scour your skin? Do you feel silky and soothed or pink and a little tingly?
- I want to you to explore the ways in which words ignite your desire. You can use this exercise in crafting short and sweet love notes, or sexy texts and emails. You can use words, or images, for your solitary pleasure.

DAY 8

SEX STARTS IN THE BRAIN

Today I want to talk about how you begin to get your brain engaged.

We use words, touch, sounds, and sight to spark the brain—to create an idea, to remember something we enjoyed, and get us in the mood for sex. By doing so we create anticipation that becomes linked with physical feelings of desire, which can help with the process of arousal. Thinking about a previous intimate encounter can be enough to start the arousal process for some.

Sexual desire often begins in our brains. We think, we feel, we see. All of our senses become involved in the process. Most of us have to be in the right mood or have the right stimulus to shift into feeling ready for sex. Feeling desire is unlikely to just "happen" and that's where the trouble starts—thinking there must be something wrong if you're not automatically in the mood when your partner is.

We've been talking about sensual experiences over the last 7 days. What's happened as you've worked through the daily exercises? What kind of thoughts are you having?

When you can begin to define the things that make you feel sexy you'll be able to tap into that state of mind, with greater ease. Awareness is crucial to any experience. Have you ever done something and want to repeat it but couldn't remember what you did the first time or how you did it? That's where awareness comes in. Sexual desire isn't a magical thing that just happens for all, or most, women and probably not consistently either. For many women the act of feeling sexual desire requires intentional effort.

In order to become engaged or excited, women need more time than men for their genitals to become aroused. We could call it the warm-up phase as long as we don't consider it a phase with a beginning and an end. Let's do away with the term "foreplay" as it suggest that stimulation is a short-term act used to prepare for sex.

For starters, it can take the average woman over 20 minutes to become fully aroused. If the attention is moved away from our genitals, arousal may be halted and we are less likely to reach maximum pleasure. Arousal and play should be a part of the complete sexual experience, not something that stops if or when a couple moves to intercourse.

When you understand that the power of memory and things that evoke memory (such as scents, sounds, and visuals) may create a desired state of mind, then you begin to develop the skills to get your brain, as well as your body, in the mood for sex. It's a bit like Pavlov's early research in behavior modification that paired the ringing of a bell with the arrival of something pleasurable (for his studies, food; for our purposes, sexual pleasure). I'm suggesting that you can begin to use your thoughts, remembering moments of intimacy, your fantasies, and whatever else you find sexy to put yourself in the mood for sex.

If only our partners understood the need to focus on our whole body—brain included. Touching, kissing, and attending to our erotic zones—other than the one between our legs—are vital to a woman's arousal process.

Daily Exercise:

- Have you ever had a kiss or a special touch from a partner that you still remember? What happens when you think about it? Can you recreate the feeling?

That is what I mean when I talk about a "sexy brain." We're tapping into our memory banks and other creative avenues to create the state of mind, that "sexy brain," which will lead to the desired physical state.

- Practice creating mental images that get you excited.
- What other things put your mind into a sexy mood?
- Make a list of things you think would help you feel desire for sex.
- You might want to also look at mood-killers. What specific things turn you off, or push you away from your partner? This list might be useful later in the book when we walk about asking for the things you want. (See Day 22)

WALKER THORNTON

DAY 9

OWNING YOUR SEXUALITY

Do women feel desire in equal measure to men? Observation of human sexuality supports this idea. Yet, research and expert opinion—from behavioral scientists, sexologists, and psychologists—show that women have a very different process when it comes to creating desire and being in the mood for sex. (1)

Every woman has her own experience of sexual desire, shaped by childhood experiences, the strength of her connection with a partner, and numerous other factors. The point I want to make is that women do have a desire for sex. Most of us want to be touched, we want to be aroused, and we want orgasms. Women are capable of passionate sex at any age! In that way we are no different from men who seek release, and pleasure, through intercourse or other means of climax. It is a physical release—something society considers quite normal, almost necessary, for a man, but not a woman.

The focus on the female orgasm hasn't always been considered a priority; in fact many women don't experience orgasms through intercourse alone, or at all. Many of us weren't raised to understand or expect that orgasms could be a normal part of sex. I'll talk about orgasms on Day 13 and again on Day 25. For older women there is an even greater cultural denial of our interest in sex. Where do we turn, what do we consider "normal" in a world that would define or restrict sexuality simply because we are women?

We start with learning to embrace our sexuality. What would happen if you invited desire into your life and made it a priority? When you embrace your sexuality, acknowledge your desires, and take regular action to find pleasure—physical or otherwise—you are taking care of yourself. You are embracing and inviting actions, sensations, and thoughts that make you feel good.

Women who embrace their sexuality are more likely to have satisfying sex lives, feel more energetic, and experience a greater degree of satisfaction in their life and in their relationship. All too often we settle for something "less than". We don't enjoy the sex we're having or we aren't having sex as often as we would like. We stay quiet (for numerous reasons) when we need to be talking about what we want or don't want.

You are choosing to take charge of your own sexuality. You made that choice by buying this book. You can make changes in your relationships, educate yourself (and your partners), and seek more satisfying sexual relationships. You can share and talk and expand your view of female sexuality in a positive, affirming way.

Obviously, you want to come to terms with your sexuality. Aren't you here because you want a more satisfying sex life? That involves embracing things you like about your sex life and taking a look at the things that aren't working for you. The first step to making any change is knowing what you want.

Daily Exercise:

- What might be different if you took full ownership of your sexuality—in and out of the bedroom? What would that look like for you? Would you dress differently, change how active or passive you are during sex? Would you want more sex? Would you end a relationship? Start dating again? Buy sex toys? Take another lover?

- Take your answers to those questions and capture them—create an erotic story, doodle, paint your thoughts, make a to-do list, or create a Vision Board. You don't have to share this with anyone. This is your exploration, your dream, of how your desired sexuality will look.

DAY 10

YOU *CAN* BE SEXUAL AND SINGLE

To think of yourself as a sexual being is first and foremost a state of mind. At any age and at any point in our lives we can become, we are, sexual beings. **We do not need a partner to make us sexual.** Learning to awaken your sexual desire is about *you* as an individual.

Granted, it's not always as much fun having sex all by yourself. But how do you define "sex"? Is sex simply the union between a man and a woman? Or is sex a wonderful intimate act providing both physical and emotional gratification that takes many forms and can involve one, two, or more individuals? Wikipedia defines human sexuality as: *the capacity to have erotic experiences and responses.* There is nothing in that definition that mentions a partner.

Sexuality need not be dictated by the conventional beliefs of our culture. We can be sexual and enjoy sexual pleasure as an individual. The single woman can have erotic experiences and responses quite happily all by herself. Sexuality is about expression and individual pleasure just as much as it is about how you experience intimate acts with another person.

Don't Limit Your Sexuality

The first 9 days of *Inviting Desire* were all about awakening your senses to the pleasures around and inside you. I want to focus on your sense of yourself as a sexual being; you are in a "relationship" with yourself first. Sex and sexuality is not—and should not be—dependent on having a partner to experience pleasure.

Whether you're between partners or don't ever intend to be sexually or romantically involved again there are still good reasons to engage in a self-pleasuring routine. These reasons include sexual health (see Day 12) and sexual pleasure.

- We feel better after a sexually satisfying experience. It's like a chemically induced high. Our bodies feel relaxed, blood flow is increased, and stress levels are reduced. Some women report a surge of sexual energy that leads to creativity and a sense of well-being.
- Arousal and orgasms contribute to sexual health, something that's particularly important for post-menopausal women. Arousal sends blood flowing to vaginal tissues, in the same way that exercise brings increased blood flow to our muscles. The activity helps to nourish and strengthen tissues in the vagina. Stronger tissues and engaged pelvic floor muscles help prevent vaginal atrophy (see Day 17 for definition). When your body is aroused, the vagina is stimulated and naturally produces lubrication, though with menopause that may vary from woman to woman. Studies typically focus on intercourse, but the key components are arousal and sexual activity, which need not involve orgasms, or partnered sex.

- Research has shown that the female orgasm produces oxytocin, a natural chemical in the body that surges before and during climax. It's sometimes referred to as the "feel good" hormone. Simply put, having orgasmic sex makes us feel good. Being in a state of pleasure, with an orgasm or not, has the same effect. (See Day 13)

- The release of oxytocin, through orgasm or sexual pleasure, helps relieve pain. According to a study by Beverly Whipple, professor emeritus at Rutgers University, sexologist, and author, when women masturbated to orgasm "the pain tolerance threshold and pain detection threshold increased significantly by 74.6 percent and 106.7 percent respectively." *(1)*

An orgasm is an orgasm, pleasurable whether self-induced or occurring during partnered sex. When you become familiar with your body, you can learn more about your preferences for touching, or being touched.

Life doesn't always present us with what we really want, when we want it, and in the exact way we planned. As strong, empowered women who understand our sexuality, we can take control of our own sexual activity to create the pleasure we desire. We don't have to wait for a partner.

So...wear your sexy clothes, watch racy movies, and read books that bring you pleasure. Experiment with sensuous activities. Be indulgent. Treat yourself as the most important person in your life. Explore all the pleasures your body has to offer you.

Daily Exercise:

- If you're not in a relationship right now, are you having regular sexual activity? If not, do you want to? What's holding you back? Think about how good it would feel to give your body a little pleasure.

- What could you do today to arouse yourself? Take five minutes, or thirty, and spend some time pleasuring yourself. Maybe you have a waterproof sex toy you can use in the shower, or you want to indulge in a sexual meditation. (See Day 20)

- Do something that turns you on—even if it's for a short period of time

- When you're finished, think about how good it felt. Why deny yourself that? And, make a promise to yourself to add stimulation and self-pleasuring to your self-care rituals. You'll be glad you did.

DAY 11

HOW WE THINK ABOUT OUR SEXUALITY

You can't start the next chapter of your life if you keep re-reading the last one.

Iyanla Vanzant (1)

What story have you made up about your sex life? About your desire for sex? Your sexuality?

The art of storytelling is a good skill, until it gets in our way. There are the public stories and there are the stories we've made up about ourselves. Those personal stories may be good, affirming, and goal-directed. But most of the time they tend to keep us from thriving or living our authentic, or true, versions of who we are.

We live in a society with few positive messages about aging or sexuality. Many women find themselves stuck in these distorted and unhealthy perceptions about female sexuality:

- Sex is only for procreation
- Menopause leaves you dried up and uninterested in sex.
- Now that I'm "Old" I'm not supposed to want sex.
- My marriage failed so I must be bad at relationships.

49

- Women aren't supposed to want to have sex.
- He's supposed to initiate sex.
- My body is too fat/saggy/ugly, too old—no one will want me.

We hear these and begin to believe them to be true about us. What have you made up about yourself? Is it an old story that haunts you or a new one, crafted to help you adjust to your current relationship with aging, your body, or your partner?

It can be difficult to look at our sexuality in a neutral, or non-biased way. We don't talk enough about healthy sexuality—at any age—to provide older women with inspiration, support, or resources to embrace their sexuality.

This was one of the driving forces behind this book. I see women who don't have the language to talk about what they want. I hear from women who have shut down their sexual selves out of fear, shame, uncertainty, or physical challenges. What often underlies these concerns and causes stumbling blocks are the stories we've made up about sex in general and about our own self-image, self-esteem, and relationships in particular.

The results of these stories can lead women to feel:

- They're no longer desirable.
- There must be something wrong with them because they can't have orgasms.
- That women who want sex are bad. Sluts.
- Their partners' erectile issues are because they aren't sexy enough.
- Menopause was difficult and fear of sex being painful has caused them to avoid sex.

- They no longer love or desire their partner but don't feel they have the right to ask for changes, or to leave an unsatisfying relationship.

In each of these cases, the woman has created a story about why it's all her fault. And it keeps her stuck in a place she doesn't really want to be—not deep down inside.

How Can You Change Your Story?

To change an old story you have to figure out what the story is, where it came from, and why you've held on to it. Part of that is understanding how that story has worked for you in the past, including those times when it hasn't been helpful.

When you figure out the story you can acknowledge it—label it and then find some compassion for yourself. You can unravel your story and look at how you embellished and fed those negative messages. And then you create new stories, almost as if you were scripting your life for a movie. Though I would caution that the key is not really to live out a story, but to live in the present, the here-and-now.

The work happens every day. The first step is awareness. The next step is to choose to let go of that story, to embrace the temporary void, and begin to create, and live, a new story for the next phase of your life.

It's a continual process of editing, deleting, and editing some more. It may require support from a counselor or therapist. You may need to retrain thought patterns, give up negative influences in your life, and work on strengthening relationships. It's not easy work. But living with a negative story your entire adult life isn't easy work either. We become so comfortable with our discomfort that we don't put energy into finding a healthier way.

I had known for a long time that I was constantly

reacting to and believing a story I had created many years ago. It was keeping me from forming healthy relationships because I was more focused on the idea that I was not "lovable." That belief led me to do what I thought men wanted, rather than the things I *wanted*.

It has only been in the last few years that I really began to dig deep and get to know my story. My big "Aha" moment came through journaling. I wrote my way to it—uncovering old messages that still banged around in my head putting me down and making me feel inadequate.

Daily Exercise:

Here are a couple of tools to help you figure out what kinds of stories, and negative messages, you have created about yourself.

- Get out a piece of paper and write down words that describe you. Then write another column with words that describe the sexual you. Be honest—do it quickly with thinking too hard. If you've got a list full of positive words, that's awesome. I'm guessing that many of you will come up with a mix of words, some of which reflect the negative feelings you carry around with you.

- Become aware of negative thoughts and statements. When are you speaking from your story? When are you reflecting the way you feel in the moment? Catch yourself telling your stories. "I doubt he'd really want to go out with someone like me." "There's something wrong with me because I can't climax with him." Where did the story come from? What's the truth about what you're experiencing? For example, if you don't orgasm is it because your partner doesn't try to pleasure you? Does he know what you like and need in order to orgasm? Or have you created a story that you can't orgasm with a certain person, or by a certain technique, and suddenly that story has become your "temporary" reality?

• Do you have a familiar story you make up about yourself, or how your partner is supposedly feeling? Speak it out loud. In front of a mirror. Exaggerate it. Embellish it. Get dramatic. See how absurd it is? Tell yourself, "This isn't my truth, it's something I created to keep me stuck, to deal with my fear," or whatever the case is for you.

The goal is to become aware of how you get caught up in stories or beliefs about yourself that aren't true. You want to recognize that moment when you begin to tell or enact the story. Then learn to change the stories—rewrite them with a positive ending. "I am a woman who enjoys sex and I have a partner who appreciates that aspect of me," or "I enjoy exploring my sexuality—and whether I'm in a relationship or not that sexual energy makes me feel great." "I get greater sexual pleasure by communicating with my partner." See how positive that is when you change the focus?

You might also want to notice those times when you "make up" some thought or opinion about your partner. So often we make assumptions about a look on someone's face or an action, and create some story about what that person is feeling—when in fact we have not checked with them to see what's really going on.

It's not as simple as it sounds. When we've lived with fear or shame or other negative emotions, letting go of those crutches can feel scary. It's a risk-taking exercise. But, it's worth the work and it's worth the sense of lightness that can come from living in the present and letting go of old stories that come with a lot of baggage.

WALKER THORNTON

DAY 12

YOUR SEXUAL HEALTH

When we talk about sexual health for older women we need to discuss more than mammograms and menopause. I think of sexual health as encompassing all aspects of our sexuality, medical and otherwise: health news, educational resources, information about intimacy and sex, and more. In a way this whole book is about female sexual health.

It's impossible to have a conversation about sexual desire without touching on women's sexual health. From the very first visit to a gynecologist, and the start of our menses, through pregnancy, to menopause, and the post-menopausal years, we are experiencing a normal sexual life cycle and, hopefully, attending to our sexual health.

Being proactive about your sexual health is no different from taking care of your teeth or getting yearly check-ups with a healthcare professional. The female body is a complex system that requires regular attention. The goal is to help you feel better physically, have satisfying sex, and understand the physical and emotional benefits of being in touch with your sexuality.

We know that aging comes with aches and pains, wrinkles, and a change in physical strength. We see it in the lines on our faces and the shifting of body parts. We rush to the gym, we get our yearly check-ups, we reach for the face potions, and yet we ignore our "lady parts."

Vaginal health is important for a number of reasons, here are two. First, the muscles of the pelvic floor, which support the bladder, get a workout during sex. The condition of our pelvic floor muscles can have an impact on bladder control. Second, sexual activity and sexual arousal stimulates blood flow to vaginal tissues, which helps keep those delicate tissues supple. Menopause, and the change in our hormone levels, result in thinning of delicate tissues—leading to a decrease in natural lubrication and the risks of tearing. As a result, some women experience discomfort during penetrative (penis in vagina) sex. (See Day 26) And in more severe cases, vaginal atrophy can occur. (See Day 17 for definition)

Vaginal health is only part of the equation when we talk about sexual health. As we've discussed throughout the book, it's what goes on in your mind that helps to create the kind of healthy sexuality you want.

Consider the conclusion from a study about older couples having sex, published in *The Journals of Gerontology* in 2014: "This study's results suggest that to protect marital quality in later life, it may be important for older adults to find ways to stay engaged in sexual activity, even as health problems render familiar forms of sexual interaction difficult or impossible." *(1)*

Intimacy provides many benefits for older adults (married or not). In addition to physical activity that benefits both females and males, sex provides us opportunities for human connection and touch. Research is beginning to show that adults who have regular intimate contact feel better about themselves and have better relationships.

British researchers recently found that men and women aged 50 to 89 who reported being sexually active experienced less cognitive decline. The researchers believe the sex hormones, like dopamine and oxytocin, contribute to greater cognitive functioning. *(2)*

A holistic approach to health requires that we look at all aspects of our lives—our physical health, our emotional health, the ways we connect with others, and our mental health. We can't ignore our sex organs just because we no longer menstruate. And we shouldn't shut down our pleasure centers just because we reach a certain age. We don't decide at some arbitrary point that we can ignore the condition of our teeth, for example. And we don't give up feeling good or wanting intimate contact in our lives when we reach midlife.

As you think about your specific needs, be sure not to ignore any medical concerns. For example, if you have issues with incontinence, discomfort in your genital area, tenderness or pain during intercourse, or other abnormalities—see the doctor. These could be possible indicators of something serious.

Daily Exercise:

Ideally you have a healthcare professional you trust and feel comfortable talking to about your sex life. Here are some things you might want to discuss:

- If you have a new sex partner, you will need to be tested for sexually transmitted infections, or diseases (STI/STD). Ask your doctor to do the testing or refer you to a testing center.
- Talk about any physical issues. Is sex uncomfortable? Does penetration hurt? Has there been any vaginal bleeding? A doctor will want to determine if the bleeding is indicative of small tears in the vaginal wall or something more serious.
- Are you experiencing bladder leakage? You can see a gynecologist who specializes in bladder issues,

often referred to as an urogynecologist. Women who worry about leaking urine may be avoiding intimacy out of embarrassment.

- If you're feeling less desire for sex are there underlying health issues? Are you on any medications that are known to affect libido? Talk to your doctor about any changes that may be impacting your interest in sex.

DAY 13

WHAT IS AN ORGASM?

What is an orgasm? Each of you will have your own experience of what an orgasm feels like for you. There isn't one standard, "this is how it feels: when we talk about orgasms. Here's how the Kinsey Institute defines them:

> "An orgasm is often defined as the peak or climax of sexual arousal. The experience of orgasm is different for everybody and from one sexual encounter to the next. Orgasms can be experienced through mental and/or physical stimulation from many different types of sexual activity...
> Physically, an orgasm can include a release of built-up muscle tension, muscle contractions in the genital and anal area, increased heart rate and faster breathing."(1)

There are different pathways to having orgasms and each woman's experience will vary. Some women can have an orgasm during intercourse, without clitoral stimulation. Others must have constant clitoral stimulation to come to a climax. And some women can have an orgasm during massage, exercise, or other stimulation of the body or the mind. There is no one definitive experience just as there is no specific way to tell you how you can have an orgasm.

In a 2015 survey of women ages 18 to 40, roughly 67 percent of respondents reported having orgasms. (2) It's probably reasonable to say that the number of women who have an orgasm every time they have sex is smaller. The reasons are complex and varied, from physiological reasons, to a partner who isn't interested in helping you achieve pleasure and everything in between.

It can be hard to define your orgasm. Some women may have quick small ripples of pleasure. It may be that your orgasm causes vaginal and anal contractions that you can feel. Your skin may flush, you may experience shaking, or other physical reactions as you climax. You might have a small intense burst of pleasure or a long slow "burn". Sometimes you're right on the edge of an orgasm—and it doesn't happen.

Try not to judge what's normal for you by listening to other people. Self-pleasuring, or masturbating, is the best way to learn about your orgasms. In those private moments you can practice how you touch yourself, how your body does or doesn't respond, and other techniques to bring more pleasure. And even then, remember that each experience is unique.

I'm not going to talk a lot about orgasms in this book because the whole "becoming orgasmic" clouds the idea of learning to feel (more) desire and increase pleasure. Regardless of age, sexual frequency, illness, disability, or many other factors, you can experience sexual pleasure in your intimate relationships, with or without an orgasm.

Daily Exercise:

- What are all the ways you imagine yourself feeling sexual pleasure? Suppose you could create a menu of options, what would be on the list? This is not about having an orgasm, but rather about specific actions that you think would feel pleasurable. Like having your scalp massaged, or your inner thighs covered in delicate kisses. A light paddling. Kissing.
- Write them down in your journal—there may come a time when you want to share this list with a partner.

WALKER THORNTON

DAY 14

SELF-PLEASURING

Today you are going to explore and play with your pleasure and arousal. Part of the process of inviting desire into your life involves learning how to find pleasure in your own body. I will be using the term "self-pleasuring", a more accurate description with none of the negative connotations associated with the term "masturbating".

We accept that men masturbate, or self-pleasure, but it's not as acceptable for women. Women tend to hold back; somehow thinking it's not OK to want to pleasure themselves. Some women may feel guilty or ashamed about touching themselves. When you don't allow yourself to find pleasure in your own body, you lose the opportunity to learn about your genitalia—knowledge that helps you experience more pleasure during sex.

This is important for you to know and accept: there is absolutely nothing wrong with self-pleasuring yourself. Forget what your parents said; forget the lessons you might have been taught as a child. If you are a woman who feels shame about sexual desire, it gets in the way of enjoying your own body and enjoying sexual intimacy.

Self-pleasuring is an important component of your sexual health plan. (See Day 12) One of the benefits of self-pleasuring is learning to embrace your sexuality as a natural thing. In doing so you give yourself permission to explore and expand your desire, which can lead to more satisfying sex with a partner.

Too often we think it's a partner's job to pleasure us. The idea that we can't satisfy ourselves is an outdated idea that limits a woman's capacity for arousal. It makes you dependent on your lover and that's a big burden for both of you. The woman who owns her desire and makes time to pleasure herself is more likely to be comfortable with her body, experience higher levels of arousal, and feel more satisfied during sex.

What will you learn through self-pleasuring?

- What and where your erogenous zones are
- What turns you on—specific spots, strokes, and thoughts
- The pace and pressure you like in sexual play
- How to bring yourself to orgasm—with fingers, toys, or a combination of the two (See Day 13)

Most importantly you will learn one of the basic steps to inviting desire into your life. You will learn that your body is desirable and capable of pleasure. You will learn to respect and love your body. And in the process, you are gathering information that can be shared with a partner who wants to provide you pleasure as well.

I doubt too many men would be upset to hear about their partner self-pleasuring herself. Some of you may have partners who will react out of insecurity— particularly if sex is mainly focused on their performance. Mostly they're fascinated and secretly want to watch. A secure partner will appreciate your ability to find pleasure in yourself and will encourage your explorations, because he understand the benefits of an awakened sexual woman.

If you feel comfortable letting a partner watch you self-pleasure it can be a powerful teaching tool, leading to better sex for both of you. By doing so you provide specific information about where and how you like to be touched. You're showing him your personal practice and you're giving him specific tips, visually or verbally (or both) depending on your comfort level. It helps him to see your personal preferences, and in so doing, teaches him how to best approach your body. You can engage on a different level from the standard "we've always done it this way" sex when you possess the knowledge of what works for you and are willing to share that knowledge.

It may feel awkward to let someone watch. Or it can be the most empowering thing you do—you may discover the hidden exhibitionist in you!

First, I urge you to play with your self-pleasuring practice alone and open yourself up to the idea of creating your own arousal. Then decide how to introduce it to your partner, or if you want to share at all. You don't have to; this is about you taking care of your own needs.

Daily Exercise:

Do you already self-pleasure? If the answer is yes, that's fabulous—do more of it. Get creative. Watch yourself in the mirror. If you're not comfortable touching yourself, start slowly.

- Start with touching your body through clothing. Caress your breasts. Place your hand over your genitals. Rock your hips back and forth while sitting in a chair. Feel how that movement brings your vulva into contact with the chair. You might feel a little tingling as your vulva and clitoris begin to become aroused. Allow yourself to respond in whatever way feels natural for you. You can just enjoy the sensation by thinking about it or you could gently stroke yourself to bring more pleasure. Tap into your senses—become aware of how your skin is responding, use your imagination to create even more arousal. Use your journal to capture the experience in words.

- Use bath time to intentionally familiarize yourself with your naked body—skip the washcloth and use your hands. Again, note the pleasurable sensations. Feel your skin come alive with your touch.

As you become more comfortable with this you can begin to practice self-pleasuring more directly. On Day 20 we'll discuss a sexual meditation, a longer more intentional way of self-pleasuring.

DAY 15

THE SEXY TOOLKIT

Over the next several days I will be talking about specific items and skills I believe are essential for your blossoming sexuality. I like to think of these as part of your sexy toolkit. This "toolkit" will contain some actual items and reflect your growing personal awareness of your ideal sexy life. Incorporating these essentials into your routines will help you invite desire into your life.

We all have helpful gadgets and bits of knowledge to assist us keep up with schedules, car repairs, work-related tasks, computer maintenance, and more. It's only natural that we develop specific tools and skills for living a sexually awakened life as well.

Here is a summary of the areas, or skillsets if you prefer, that a sexy toolkit might include. In the next few days we will look at specific tools for arousal:

Body Knowledge: Learning what arouses you, where you want to be touched, what feels good, and what you want or need.

A Self-Pleasuring Practice: You spend time indulging in sensuous practices and self-pleasuring. (See Day 14) Maybe you are adopting a regular sexual meditation routine. (See Day 20) You think about your sexual health and wellness, and incorporate that knowledge in your self-care rituals.

Tools for Arousal: You are gathering clothing and accessories that can be used to enhance your desire. (See Day 16) You understand the benefits of using lubrication. (See Day 17) There is a sex toy in your toolkit—maybe more than one. (See Day 18)

Communication Skills or Tools: Communication with partners is an on-going process. We never stop communicating, in and out of the bedroom. Being clear about what you need emotionally as well as physically is crucial. You are learning to ask for what you want. And to talk about what you might be willing to do. (See Day 22)

Daily Exercise:

- Imagine you have a pretty little chest or "toolbox." Later you might want to buy a real chest or box for storing your essentials and your toys. I want you to begin filling your imaginary toolbox with all the things that you find exciting, items that feel sensuous, erotic, or sexual to you. Collect pictures you find appealing—people, places, and exotic landscapes. Build a library of music to awaken and ignite. Add colors, sketches, or snippets of verse. If something inspires you, grab it. Embrace it.

- You can use a Pinterest board, a Vision Board, or journal to gather things for your future toolkit. Think about the colors, textures, and images that speak to your sensuous side. Add images that arouse or stimulate you. Where would you like to have sex? On the beach or on a bed of moss? Collect pictures of those sites. What makes you feel sexy? Silky Egyptian cotton sheets? Beautiful candles? Are there sensuous photos or drawings of bodies, sex positions, or romantic couplings that you like? Collect them. The images will serve as a reminder of how you envision your sexy self.

WALKER THORNTON

DAY 16

LINGERIE

Your sexy toolkit should include at least one piece of lingerie or erotic clothing that makes you feel like a Goddess and as sexy as hell. Consider a sexy nightgown, a lacy bra and panty set, thigh-high hose. A corset, nipple jewelry...the possibilities are endless.

The first step in picking out new lingerie is to consider your goal, or desired look. Are you looking for a new nightgown that's slightly racy or a wildly seductive outfit? Do you want to role-play or act out fantasies (for example, the French Maid, or the Nurse)? Are you buying something just for you or to wear for a lover?

You want to feel comfortable in your new outfit—I don't advise you to go straight from flannel PJs to a red satiny number with nipple cutouts. A gown with lace details or thin spaghetti straps and a lower neckline might be a good choice for the newly adventurous. Choose something that makes you feel good.

Is there such a thing as "age-appropriate" when it comes to lingerie? No...maybe. The important thing is to pick an outfit that makes *you* feel sexy. If you can rock a sexy little babydoll outfit, go for it.

What's your favorite style? Frills and lace, plain and tailored, hot and naughty? There is something for everyone. From frilly, girlie outfits that offer confectionery-like appeal to black 'leather' with studs, zippers, and chains. If you prefer the sophisticated, classic look you'll find that too.

If this is a new experience for you, you might be surprised by the selection at your local department store. There are chain stores like Victoria's Secret as well as high-end lingerie boutiques. Internet shops run from stylish boutiques, to websites for sex-positive communities, to triple-X rated porn sites, and everything in between. An online shop is more likely to carry larger sizes than local boutiques. You may sacrifice the ability to try something on, for the anonymity of shopping from home.

Decide which piece of lingerie to buy first. There are plenty of options, depending on your goal and how much money you want to spend. You can always add to your collection as you get more daring. Here are some ideas to start with:

- Nightgown
- Panties— lacy, boy-cut, wild colors, thongs
- A teddy or one-piece to wear alone or under an outfit
- A sexy new bra—embroidered, push-up, demi-cup, sheer
- Lacy camisole to wear alone or for layering
  Unbutton a few buttons and let the lace-edging peek out under your blouse, sweater, or jacket.
- Role-playing outfits—French Maid, Schoolgirl, Nurse, Dominatrix…

I can hear you now, "But my body is (fill in the blank)." We're not going to play that game; for too long our culture has pushed the notion that beauty equals young and thin. Beauty is internal and every age presents us with opportunities to shine.

Remember, your body is a beautiful thing and reflective of the life you've lived. You can choose lingerie to emphasize or downplay features as you wish. A gown with a fitted bodice gives shape and support to breasts. Want to show off your curves? Wear a form fitting gown or a corset.

You can be more daring with panties and pair them with a less revealing top. Think sexy white panties with a tailored white shirt. A matching bra and panty set. Animal print thongs under a business suit.

Sheer lingerie is probably best for the woman who is comfortable baring it all. The anticipation and sex appeal of a well-draped body can be just as exciting as a naked one. A hint of skin, the curve of a breast, the soft sway of hips as you walk in a flowing outfit are incredibly seductive and alluring.

If sexy lingerie feels a little scary to you there are less revealing options. Consider a long flowing nightgown, dress, or caftan. A hint of cleavage or a glimpse of a lacy camisole beneath a blouse or sweater can be pretty enticing. When your partner sees you in your new sexy outfit he won't notice what you might consider a flaw!

Don't be put off if your favorite lingerie shop or website doesn't feature older or plus-sized models in their advertisements; that's no reason to think you can't carry off sexy lingerie. You can wear anything you want.

Daily Exercise:

- You're going lingerie shopping, but first I want you to go on a fantasy shopping trip. Go to your local department store or an online lingerie boutique and browse. Think about what piece of lingerie you want to start with. Do you want a lacy camisole, black silk nightie, bra and panty set, or a corset? Look through the selections and think about what piece might be fun for you. What will make you feel sexy and confident?

- The next step is to actually go shopping. You've narrowed down the choices and have some idea of what piece of lingerie you want. Now, purchase it. This isn't simply an indulgence—this is an essential for your sexy life. This is self-care. This is you tapping into your sensuousness.

DAY 17

LUBRICANTS

A lubricant, or lube, is one of those essentials that every sexual woman should have in her toolkit. Essential at any age, lubricants help provide more pleasure by enhancing sensation and eliminating uncomfortable friction. Think of lube as a sex toy. (I'll discuss sex toys on Day 18.)

The silky satiny feeling of a good lubricant enhances the experience. Dry fingers create drag as they move across skin, the exact opposite of the smooth sensation you want as a part of a sexual experience. Using a lubricant during sex allows fingers, toys, and other body parts to glide over skin.

Menopause and Lubrication

There are plenty of articles about lube and older women and the focus is always on lubricant as a helpful, or necessary, aid in intercourse. I agree. But, for our purposes we are going to talk about sexual pleasure, not just intercourse.

Using a lubricant with any kind of sex play or self-pleasuring is important. The clitoris has about 8,000 nerve endings and can be sensitive to touch. Lubricant helps creates a gentle smooth touch as you or your lover play with your clitoris and the surrounding area. (See Figure 1.)

Vaginal dryness can be an issue at any age and may be caused by various factors. Stress, side effects of certain medications, and the lack of arousal often contribute to vaginal dryness. The hormonal changes that occur during menopause can cause a woman's natural lubrication to lessen over time. For some women dryness is not an issue, and for others it leads to discomfort and, in extreme cases, pain during penetration.

Here's how The North American Menopause Society explains the loss of lubrication: "During perimenopause, less estrogen may cause the tissues of the vulva and the lining of the vagina to become thinner, drier, and less elastic or flexible—a condition known as *"vulvovaginal atrophy."* Vaginal secretions are reduced, resulting in decreased lubrication." *(1)*

Choosing a Good Lubricant

Inviting desire into your life is about creating moments of pleasure and nurturing your sensuous side. The goal of this book is to assist you in learning to give yourself pleasure and to enhance your feeling of yourself as a sexual woman. You need tools to help you along in your journey—a lubricant that is safe for your body is one of those tools. Think of using lubricant on equal par with applying a good eye cream.

There are water-based, oil-based, and silicone-based lubricants. The choice is a personal one, which should take into consideration your skin's sensitivity to scents and additives, personal preferences, and whether you're using condoms and sex toys.

- Water-soluble lubricants are easily absorbed into the skin, so they may have to be reapplied during play. They are safe for use with condoms or silicone sex toys.

- Oil-based lubricants should not be used with latex condoms. They can weaken the latex and cause the condom to break.
- Silicone-based lubricants last longer and tend to be more slippery than water-based ones. They may be safe for use with some silicone-based toys but not with others—read the manufacturer's instructions.

There are plenty of options for buying lubricants, as close as your grocery or drug store. Some of the online websites have a great selection of lubricants you can order with ease and discretion. (See Endnotes for suggestions.) *(2)*

Read the labels carefully; many of the popular brands contain additives and chemicals that you don't want to use on sensitive genital tissues. I suggest purchasing all-natural or organic lubricants, such as organic almond oil or coconut oil—both available at your local grocery store.

My toolkit contains an organic coconut oil, two organic water-based products, and a silicone lubricant. I don't use flavored lubricants but some people love them as a way of camouflaging natural scents. You will want to find the right match for your tastes and sexual preferences.

Daily Exercise:

Set aside some play time with your new lubricant. The goal of this exercise is to feel pleasure; you aren't necessarily trying to achieve an orgasm. I want you to feel and understand the benefits of using a lube. Use it to caress your nipples. Put it on your fingers and begin to explore and caress your genitals—your labia, clitoris, and the entrance to your vagina. Feel how your fingers glide, without tugging the skin, in an even, smooth movement. If you use a sex toy, use the water-based lubricant with it. You can put a few drops on the toy (preferable) or lube up your vulvar region. Again, pay attention to how much smoother and sensuous your body feels with lubricant.

DAY 18

SEX TOYS

Sex toys are a blessing for human sexuality. They are not crutches, nor are they substitutes for anything and they are here to stay.

-Betty Dodson (1)

Though fingers, lips, tongues, and other body parts are delicious when it comes to creating pleasure, sometimes using a sex toy can add to the experience. Simply put, a sex toy can be defined as any object or device designed just for the purpose of creating or enhancing sexual pleasure.

Sex toys vary in quality, materials, safety, and design. Today there is a wide range of products available, all of which fall under the broad category of sex toys.

These include items like cushions and wedges for more comfortable positioning; vibrating tools to massage or stimulate; and even kinkier items such as ropes and handcuffs, paddles, nipple clamps, and much more. For our purposes we are going to focus on vibrators—a good all-purpose first toy if you're new to the idea. (See Day 15)

I think every woman needs at least one sex toy in her

toolbox. They are a wonderful enhancement to self-pleasuring. Sex toys can be used with a partner for added clitoral stimulation, or on other body parts, bringing variety and excitement to self-pleasuring. But what toy to buy? How do you figure out what works for you?

There are many types of vibrators to choose from. You will find small (pocket vibrators) to large penis-shaped ones, and everything in between.

There are G-spot vibrators, clitoral vibrators, waterproof vibrators, the Rabbit, the Magic Wand, and the list goes on and on.

Let's assume you've never used a vibrator. Maybe you don't think you need one. This is not about *need* even though I think every woman needs a vibrator. I want you to experiment with vibrators because they can help awaken your body and help you learn more about *your* arousal process. Using a vibrator is about giving yourself pleasure—on and around the clitoris, the vulva, at the opening to your vagina (the introitus), in your vagina—wherever you want to stimulate your body. (See Figure 2)

Let's Talk About Types of Vibrators

The basic vibrator is long and slender, and is designed for both external and internal use. Vibrators are available in a variety of shapes and sizes and every imaginable color, shape, and price range. Start with one and then add to your collection as you gain experience. You can find vibrators at a variety of stores, online, and locally. I've listed a few of the reputable online sex toy shops in the Endnotes. *(2)*

Vibrator Types:

Pocket Vibrators: These might be called small, mini, or discreet vibrators. The Pocket Rocket is another popular term. One of the things I love about the compact vibrators is that they are small enough to literally put in your pocket and take anywhere. And, small enough for you or a partner to use along with another form of sexual activity.

Think about the possibilities for using a vibrator while receiving oral or manual stimulation during intimate play. A small vibrator fits nicely between two bodies during intercourse to provide clitoral stimulation.

The Rabbit-Type Vibrator: Thanks to an episode in the television series *Sex and The City*, this toy has grown in popularity. The rabbit typically feature two separate controls, one for the rabbit ears, and the other for the rotation and speed of the penis-shaped vibrator. Near the base of the shaft there is a section that holds pearl-like beads, which rotate, creating another sensation when the toy is inside the vagina. When the shaft is inserted into the vagina, the ears of the rabbit come into contact with the clitoris. The distance from the vaginal opening to the clitoris varies for each woman so you might have to adjust the position of toy to make it work for you. This is primarily a solo play toy.

G-Spot Vibrators: Do we have a G-spot? Probably (there is some debate, even among the experts as to whether it exists and whether women can have G-spot orgasms), but not all women respond to G-spot stimulation. This type of vibrator is curved up slightly at the tip to allow for positioning on the G-spot deep within the vagina. If you've never had an orgasm this might not be the first vibrator you buy.

Deluxe Vibrators: Jimmyjane, Lelo, Crave, and We-Vibe are a few of the high-end companies designing sex toys today. A sheer pleasure to look at, they offer more features, have stronger motors, are made of better quality materials (silicone, metals or glass), and look sleek and sexy. Pricy, but worth it!

The key to using vibrators is your willingness to experiment. With your favorite water-based lubricant and a desire to pleasure yourself, you can accomplish a couple of things. (See Day 17)

- You can build arousal: engaging your mind and body in sexual activities has the effect of making you want more.
- You can increase your sexual response by learning what turns you on.
- You can practice becoming orgasmic, if you choose. Not all women have orgasms, so it's important to be attuned to pleasure in a broader sense. (See Day 13)
- You can explore your body to identify your erotic spots, an important part of becoming orgasmic. You may be surprised to find pleasure where you least expect it.
- You will feel more relaxed and less stressed after a good session of self-pleasuring. Research has shown that the hormone oxytocin is released during pleasure.

Many partners are turned on by the idea of a woman who owns sex toys. It means she's interested in her sexual arousal. It's rare that a man feels threatened by a woman who uses sex toys, but it can happen. Just explain that this is not a replacement for him but a tool to enhance enjoyment for you and consequently for him. Then suggest he try it out with you. Your partner could use a sex toy on your clitoris or surrounding areas (nipples enjoy stimulation too) or use it during oral or penetrative sex to enhance the experience for both of you.

Think about the vibrator as an addition to your sexual repertoire—you still want to engage in regular self-touch and other activities to bring pleasure and maybe orgasms. (See Day 14) You don't want to get so dependent on a vibrator that you can't achieve orgasms in other ways. Strive for variety.

Daily Exercise:

- I want you to buy a vibrator. Get an inexpensive one if you're not sure how you feel about using a vibrator. Once you see how much fun and useful sex toys are you'll probably want to get a nicer one. Don't buy a sex toy made with phthalates. (3)

- Once you get your vibrator you are going to set aside an hour to get acquainted with your new toy. See how it feels, explore, test it out. Most vibrators have several speeds and types of vibrations—see what you like. Don't forget to use a water-based lube.

- If you're new to this, go slow when applying the vibrator directly to your clitoris. The clitoris, or clit, can be hypersensitive. Use the vibrator lightly on the hood of the clit and around the sides.

- As you use the vibrator to caress your body, pay attention to what feels pleasurable. Is there one spot that feels better than others? Are there places where the vibration doesn't feel as good? How fast or intense do you like your vibrations? Does varying the speed or intensity feel good? These distinctions are important to note and provide valuable feedback, which you can then share with a lover. Don't forget that your preferences can change over time, so you might want to experiment occasionally.

DAY 19

FLIRTING

It's not what I do, but the way I do it. It's not what I say, but the way I say it.

-Mae West

Flirting doesn't come naturally to everyone, but that doesn't mean you can't learn how. Flirting is a way of interacting with a person you find attractive. You can flirt to convey your interest in another person, as a playful gesture or as a prelude to sex. It's appropriate in many situations and with most people you find appealing.

Consider flirting as a form of play. You might flirt with your partner as a way of getting his attention, or to indicate your desire for sex. Flirting can be helpful in getting you in the mood. The sexually charged interchange with your partner or a person you find attractive provides a boost that helps you feel confident and sexy.

At its most basic level, flirting is a playful way of interacting and of signaling your interest in someone you find interesting.

The Key Components of Flirting

Eye Contact: Make eye-to-eye contact with the person

you're flirting with. It's not something we do often enough, but it can be powerful in a good way, even though as women many of us were taught not to be quite so direct. The directness lets that person know you're looking, or listening, and interested in him. If you see someone across the room who looks appealing, catch his eye and smile at him. That lets him know you've seen him and find him attractive. Let him catch you looking a second time.

Body Language: Our body language reveals a lot about us. Crossed arms send a "don't mess with me" signal. An open body, arms at your side or in your lap, shows that you're relaxed and welcoming. Give him visual cues by leaning in and facing him directly with your body and face. Gestures such as caressing your arm or touching your face show you're interested. You are sending a signal. Obviously when you touch yourself, smoothing your hands down your dress, or touching your neck, his eyes will be drawn to your body. There are plenty of gestures typically used in flirting; some of which may seem a little "girlish" for an older woman. For example, twirling your hair. Do what feels natural for you.

Touch: Touching another person is a powerful way of connecting. You can touch a man casually on the wrist during a conversation or lightly place your hand on his arm. This kind of subtle touch allows you to establish a more immediate physical connection. If you get up from the table or walk by him in a crowded room, a light touch on the shoulder or back, with an "excuse me" will get his attention. Touching his chest or leg might be interpreted as a more intimate gesture, an invitation perhaps.

Conversation: Look at him directly, give him your full attention and really listen. Use facial gestures to reinforce your listening—a nod, a murmur of agreement. Engage him; ask about his work, his interests, or hobbies. Everyone loves to be listened to. It shows respect, interest, and gives your partner a sense of self-worth. It's a great way to let someone know you care.

Flirting is a tool you can use to your advantage. Figure out what feels comfortable for you and the level of interaction you want with the person you are flirting with. Trust your intuition. If it feels safe, you can go farther and become more explicitly sexual.

Desire isn't something that has an expiration date. We are sexy and desirable if we see ourselves as such. You can show that in actions, words, and your intention when you engage possible partners. Being flirtatious gives you permission to be a little adventurous when it comes to sex.

Sometimes it's not about sex at all, just mutual appreciation.

Daily Exercise

- If flirting feels uncomfortable for you, start out by watching others flirt. You can start slowly. When you talk to the produce guy or the letter carrier, or that nice-looking person in line behind you, look them in the eye and flash a big smile. Tap into your feminine side and see what kind of reaction you get. If you're nervous, ask a friend to practice with you.

- If you are in a relationship, what role would flirting play? Is it a playful icebreaker, or an "I'm in the mood" message? You can flirt through emails and texts as well—it's a great way to get things heated up before a date.

WALKER THORNTON

DAY 20

A SEXUAL MEDITATION

A regular meditation practice helps to reduce stress, calm our bodies, lower blood pressure, and become more connected with our inner selves. A sexually focused meditation *(1)* can provide some of those same benefits, as it helps you refocus your energies and increase your ability to bring about arousal.

The practice I'm going to describe can be incorporated into your daily or weekly routine. Just as with traditional meditation, you want to set up your surroundings, eliminate distractions, and find a comfortable position. This sexual exploration, or meditation, as I like to call it, is about connecting with your body in a non-judgmental, exploratory fashion.

The goal is to explore your erogenous areas—the parts of your body that, when touched, respond sexually—focusing exclusively on touch.

Think of this as a mix of self-pleasuring and meditation. There are many people teaching orgasmic meditation or tantric meditation—this is something different. It is an intentional way to awaken the body, explore, and enhance your body's responsiveness to touch. This is a solo practice—just for you, to be done in your own home. This is not an exercise for your partner to explore with you—not yet, at least.

When you awaken your body by respecting and paying

attention to it, you are validating your sexuality. This is beyond self-care; this is self-love.

I believe that we become more sexually responsive by getting to know our own bodies. As you identify the sensations that awaken your skin you are learning about your erotic zones. You will feel the physical changes brought about by blood flow to your vulva and vaginal tissues. You will feel your clitoris swell and grow hard under your touch. You will discover which kinds of touch you like.

Many of us bought into the myth that only young bodies are sexy and that mind-blowing orgasms happen spontaneously. This exercise will allow you to learn more about your own body and its capacity for pleasure. This practice of loving touch allows you to discover the beauty of your vulva, labia, and clitoris. You are experiencing your body on your terms. And as you learn your body's responses to touch you are opening the way to greater sexual pleasure—single or partnered.

To learn more about the female anatomy see the Figures.

Daily Exercise:

- Give yourself at least 30 minutes of uninterrupted alone time. Set up your bedroom with comfortable temperature and lighting. You should be completely undressed. Get settled on your bed. You want your knees bent with legs falling open, using pillows under your legs for support. This position should feel comfortable and fully support your legs. Use a lubricant—it's important to this process. Organic coconut oil is my go-to lube for this. (See Day 17)
- Begin to slowly caress your body, starting at your breasts and working down. Lightly apply lube to

hands. Use soft, slow strokes down and across your body. Try different types of strokes to see what feels best.

- As you move towards your genitals, caress your inner thighs as you move to the outside of the labia. Then the inside of the labia; notice how each area feels when touched. Caress around, above and on your clitoris. Use movements that move the skin across the top of the clitoris. (See Figure 1)

- Some women have a very sensitive clitoris and don't enjoy direct stimulation. Is that true for you? You might like a gentle tapping on your clitoris and labia. Experiment to find what you like and don't like. Add more lubricant as needed. Stroke and touch as long as it feels pleasurable to you. Stay focused on your movements. Note what feels good but don't get stuck analyzing the sensations.

- You are paying tribute to your body, pleasuring it. Adoration and acknowledgment and self-care all wrapped up in one. Take it slow and intentional— there is no goal for this exploration. You are not trying to have an orgasm; you are simply caressing and exploring your body.

Experiment with this sexual meditation at least once a week—more if you feel moved to do so. It's a wonderful way to start the day, or end a stressful one. You will begin to notice your arousal patterns and the accompanying changes in your body. You may experience great pleasure or simply a gentle, nice feeling. Touching your genitals brings increased blood flow, heightened awareness, an easing of tensions, and an understanding of your arousal patterns.

This might be a good exercise to journal about—noting how various strokes feel, the ease of getting in a rhythm, what calms you and what arouses you. Write down any discoveries and any ideas you might want to share with a partner later.

DAY 21

CREATING THE RIGHT ENVIRONMENT FOR SEX

What do you need in order to be comfortable during sex? What does your ideal sexual encounter look like? In particular, do you have specific ideas about how you want to set up your bed or your room?

Let's face it; we're not as young as we used to be. Maybe your knees, or hips, not to mention your lower back, won't allow you to get in some positions. Are there limitations that get in the way of having sex like you did in your 20s? You need to be comfortable in order to have a satisfying sexual experience.

What Do You Need In Order To Have Comfy Sex?

I bet no one has ever asked you that question! Think about it. What little quirks do you have in the bedroom? For example, I have bouts of vertigo, so I need a small pillow under my head. Your particular needs could be about room temperature, lighting, position, or sound. There are logistical and atmospheric conditions that can impact how comfortable you are during sex and therefore make sex more pleasurable.

Room temperature: If you have frequent hot flashes does the room temperature need to be cooler? A ceiling fan is great for creating gentle breezes but not so great during sex if it contributes to dryness. Do you or your partner have a preference when it comes to temperature?

Lighting: As older women there may come a time when we become less comfortable with our bodies. Ideally you would be comfortable revealing the beauty of your body to a partner. You may not realize that your partner appreciates what he's seeing, even when you don't. Our cultural conditioning can be strong, so if you feel uncomfortable in full light do what's necessary to feel more at ease.

Dim lighting adds atmosphere while reducing harsh glare. Light candles or dim the lights to create a romantic mood. If you like having sex with the lights out that's fine too. Make sure to state your preferences to your partner so you can both be comfortable. You can turn off the room light and use light from an adjoining room to see what you're doing, allowing for non-verbal communication.

Beds: Position is important for both of you. Do you need a pillow under your head? Are you lying in a position on the bed that allows both bodies to be fully supported? Do you use pillows or wedges to elevate your hips to increase sexual pleasure? (See Endnotes for ideas) (1) Performing oral sex on a woman can cause a strain on the giver's neck, which can be lessened by changing positions. You can slide to the edge of the bed so he can kneel on the floor (if his knees can handle it) or lie side by side, in a modified "69" position. You might experiment with positions to find something that works for you.

Coverings: We no longer have sex in our pajamas, under the covers, with eyes tightly closed, but there are times when a little covering might help you feel less exposed and, therefore, sexier. A sheet or light throw can be used for a little draping before or after sex. For a sexy, but less revealing look, you can wear a lacy camisole, panty-less, while having sex. Think creatively here. Drape or not, clothed or nude—it's up to you to figure out what will allow you to relax and maintain your focus.

Sounds: Do sounds help or distract? Do you want music to shut out outside noises? If so what do you like? Nature sounds, or something with a rhythm? I find songs distracting—you may discover that music adds to your experience. Think about what you like and then check in with your partner to see if he has strong feelings.

It's Your Pleasure—Enhance It!

This is about your sexual pleasure. Experiment to figure out what you like. If the room atmosphere is important to you, buy some sexy sheets for the bed. Get a new candle. Replace the cotton pillowcases with silky ones. Get the music ready and volume adjusted ahead of time. Get a silky scarf or necktie and drape it over the headboard, then ask him if he'd be interested in trying something playful. Wear a teddy to bed and have your partner undress you or figure out how to make love to you while you're wearing it.

The goal is two-fold. You want to feel comfortable and safe when you have sex. But at the same time you might want to step out of your normal, everyday routine. Get a little wild. Have fun!

Daily Exercise:

- Think back to times when you've been uncomfortable during sex, physically or otherwise. What was missing? What addition or change would have made things better, easier, more comfortable? What could you say next time to make it work for you?
- Daydream about your next sexual encounter. What do you want to happen? What will you need to add in order to create that atmosphere? You might even send your lover an email, or text telling him what you're planning—to further enhance the excitement for both of you.
- Before having sex take a few minutes to set up your room. Place the lube by the bed; get out your favorite sex toy, and maybe a towel. Do you need a pillow to elevate your hips? Music ready? What else do you want to have at your fingertips?

Having everything in place adds to the mood and lets your partner know that you've been thinking about how to maximize the enjoyment of your time together. Think of this as a ritual that helps to get you in the mood. Desire begins in the brain and the simplest of acts become associated with something—in this case, your desire for sex.

DAY 22

LEARNING TO ASK FOR WHAT YOU WANT

You've spent the last 21 days nurturing yourself and your body, and thinking about the idea of inviting desire into your life. You can learn how to increase your sense of desire and you can learn to feel desire as it shows up in your body. But in order to reach the fullest sense of desire as you engage in intimacy with another person you have to be willing to ask for what you want. You want a change. This book is hopefully encouraging you to read, practice and think about desire as it shows up in your life.

Here's what I think we weren't taught as women: You are responsible for your own sexual satisfaction. Betty Dodson (1) says this—it's beautifully simple yet very difficult to achieve if you're not used to speaking up for yourself.

What Does It Mean to Ask For What You Want?

- It means that you have to take an active role in creating the kind of sexual satisfaction you hope to achieve. You will need to work with your partner to create sexual activity that is pleasurable for you, and for them. It means understanding that men don't automatically know what to do with our beautifully complex bodies. It's not fair for either of you if you're silently expecting a partner to know exactly what you want.

- It means you get to help your partner discover your body and what turns you on. If you don't have a partner then you get to learn new and delightful ways to satisfy yourself.

Growing up in a time when "good girls" weren't supposed to have sex, we didn't learn much about sex or our bodies. And, we depended on our male partners to show us what sex was all about. They were the experienced ones. What we're learning is that the key to a pleasurable sex life involves taking responsibility for getting what we want and need.

Your journey to invite desire into your life can't be accomplished alone—you have to learn how to involve partners, and you have to learn to use your voice when it comes to sex. Whether you are in a relationship or have a lover, one of the keys to having better sex is becoming comfortable in asking for what you want. On Day 23 I'll address relationships where sexual activity has shut down.

Getting your needs met and having your wishes heard and respected will strengthen your relationship, and all of those things work to increase your sexual pleasure. Let's look at how you can start a conversation about your sexual wants and needs.

We forget that our partners aren't mind readers. If he isn't giving you what you need it might be because he hasn't a clue as to what that is. It is your job to convey your wishes to him and in some cases show him exactly what that means. I can't emphasize that enough—we are responsible for making sure we get the kinds of stimulation that we want or need.

Many women aren't comfortable speaking up. We weren't taught how to ask for things, especially not when it comes to sex. Asking for what you want may feel scary and difficult so I'm going to give you a few conversation starters:

- "I was reading an article the other day about ways to add a little extra zip to your sex life. I'd like to try something new." Then talk about something you want to try, like: "We've never tried giving each other massages. Would you give me a back/foot/scalp massage?"
- "I found a sexy movie I'd like us to watch together. Let's plan a movie date-night." Be sure to set a specific date right then.
- "I don't know what came over me, but I went shopping today and bought a sexy little bra with matching panties. Want me to model them for you? The thought of that gets me a little aroused. You?"
- "I loved it when you [describe how: gently, firmly, teasingly, with fingernails, etc.] touched me on my insert body part the other night. Can I show you other places that turn me on?
- "I'm feeling naughty. I found this old tie of yours— wonder what it would feel like to be tied up while you kiss me all over"
- "Remember when I mentioned that sometimes I feel like I'm not wet enough when you start to enter me? I bought some lube! It feels really nice on my skin. I gave it a test run this afternoon while thinking about you. Let's try it."
- "I've had this dream about something I'd like you to do to, or with, me. May I share it?"
- Lunchtime text to your partner: "Was thinking of you so I got out my new vibrator. Fun. Come home

early and I'll show you how I like to use it. Might let you try it…"

You have the power to change your sexual relationship. All it takes is a little daring and a willingness to experiment. What's holding you back?

Daily Exercise:

- Pick one of the suggestions above, or create your own, and try asking for something you want. If speaking up feels too uncomfortable, write a note. The request doesn't have to be about sex at all; you could ask for a foot rub, or to hold hands. The goal is to practice talking about and asking for the things that give you pleasure. Don't wait until you get to the bedroom to do this. Talk about what you want in a neutral place. This lets you decide what you want to try before you are in the middle of the action, and might be too nervous to stop if you are feeling uncomfortable. While you can change your mind at any time, having a plan first is always helpful.

DAY 23

WHAT IF YOU'RE NO LONGER HAVING SEX?

On Day 22 we talked about communicating specific sexual wants, based on the assumption that you and your partner are having sex. But, what if you've stopped having sex altogether? What if there is no intimacy at all in your relationship?

How will you start that communication? Some level of communication will be necessary—and what it looks like will be based on the current level of intimacy and communication you have with your partner. The couple that hasn't had sex in 8 months, or 8 years, is in a different place than the couple that is having sex and wants to make some changes.

My suggestions are geared towards creating the right communication for your unique situation, but remember that I am not a licensed counselor. You may want to consider counseling as an option—either traditional couples counseling or specialized work with a sex therapist (suggestions below).

If you're ready to reconnect with your partner how do you start? What do you need to communicate about the things you've learned from reading this book and doing the daily exercises? What do you need him to hear and what do you want him to do? This is not the place or time for a vague talk about wanting sex again. You've been learning about your body and thinking about how you want to be touched—about the kind of intimacy you desire.

What steps can you take to add intimacy to your relationship again? It's rarely as simple as saying, "I'm ready to have sex again." You might want to start with more general conversation about your relationship. The answer is very individual; I can't tell you exactly what to do, but I can offer some ideas and tips on communicating.

Regardless of the topic, when you need to talk about something that is complex and emotionally charged it's best to start the conversation calmly and in a neutral place. Pick a time when you feel your partner would be most receptive to the conversation. Ask if he is ready to talk about it. You might think he's receptive when he's really not. It can be difficult when one person in a relationship begins to change; as things shift the partner may feel threatened. They may have created some story that it's all about them, when this is really about your journey to become more attuned to your body. Regardless, you want to be considerate of your partner's feelings.

Plan that first conversation—when you'll initiate it, and what you want to say. It might be helpful to set some ground rules if you're not use to having the kind of conversations where difficult emotions and topics are discussed. What do you want him to do, or not do? Be very clear and specific; it will help avoid any unspoken expectations. For example, "I want to share what's been going on with me. And I want you to just listen first." (See Endnotes for more information about having difficult conversations.) *(1)*

It's not unusual to experience some resistance. One or both of you may feel nervous about having the conversation, not to mention the idea of beginning to reconnect sexually. Take baby steps. And don't expect one conversation to fix everything. You are making changes in how you relate to your body and those personal changes also change the dynamic of your relationship.

This could take time. Go at a pace that feels right for you. Remember this is about you reconnecting with your body, and your needs and desires.

Both of you have to want sexual intimacy for this to work. You may have differing levels of enthusiasm or readiness, but both of you have to be willing to try. When you both decide you are ready, you want to take it slowly, with agreed upon steps. Some couples might be able to have one conversation and head right to the bedroom. The more likely scenario is that one of you begins talking about what you want to happen. Then the two of you come up with a plan for reestablishing intimacy.

In the Endnotes you will find books on the topic of healthy relationships and couple counseling. *(2)* You can choose couples counseling or you could work with a sex therapist. AASECT (American Association of Sexuality Educators, Counselors, and Therapists) has a link on their website to help you locate the nearest certified sex therapists—https://www.aasect.org/referral-directory.

Daily Exercise:

I would suggest that you do some preliminary work in preparation for the conversation with your partner. Think about your answer to these questions. You might want to write them down and actually refer to your notes when you talk to your partner.

- How is your relationship in general? And how will that affect your ability to have these conversations?
- What do you want to happen in your sexual relationship? Do you want to start having sex again or do you just want a little more attention and affection?
- Does he want sex? How comfortable is he talking about sex?
- Do either of you have any physical issues, such as illness, aches and pains, or medications that might interfere with desire or arousal?

Now comes the second part: this involves thinking about what you want in the way of intimate contact. Here are some possibilities—think about what you want and how to share that with your partner. Part of the conversation should include how one of you asks to slow down or stop if things feel uncomfortable. Think about how you will honor each other's feelings.

- Do you want to start by holding hands while watching a movie?
- A hug or kiss when you leave for work or get home in the evening?
- Cuddling in bed.
- Take turns making suggestions as to what might be fun tonight.

DAY 24

THE PRACTICE OF SAYING YES...OR NO

Have you ever agreed to have sex with a partner, knowing you didn't really want to, but were giving in for some reason? You said yes, with (unspoken) reservations. Your ambivalence, detachment, or resentment—whatever emotion that might go along with that reluctant "yes"— creates a lack of desire, which over time could result in you avoiding intimacy.

Being able to comfortably say yes, or no, is crucial to inviting desire into your life. When you invite something into your life you've made a choice to welcome that thing, to find enjoyment in the experience. Ambivalence can shift to a more enthusiastic attitude if you are open to possibilities. There may be times when you agree to sex even if you're a bit uncertain. By telling your partner how you're feeling, you leave open the possibility of changing your mind. And that's a legitimate place to be. But if you're always ambivalent about having sex maybe you need to figure out what's getting in the way of your pleasure.

When you say yes and make a conscious decision to have sex, you give yourself permission to get excited, to prepare, to be flirty or sultry. You do whatever you need to do to make the experience pleasurable. Because you said yes you're not going to show up with a borderline attitude. Your experience will be much more fun if you have an open, receptive attitude. Though remember, you always have the option to change your mind if something changes or you become uncomfortable.

It's more fun for our partners when we show up as a willing participant. We're more likely to have greater sexual pleasure when our mind is engaged, along with our body. We are more excited about being with our partner and that feeling communicates itself. All around, it's better—this idea of fully embracing our sexual moments.

Let's look at saying yes and how it might lead to a more fulfilling sex life—whether you're partnered or solo. There are legitimate times when you want to say no and that's normal. It's actually very healthy for relationships if you can communicate what you want in any given moment. The process of being able to say yes requires you to think about what you like about your current sexual activity and what you don't like. Is there something you're currently doing that feels more like a "Maybe"? If you're not sure consider it a "No" for now, until you're ready for a heartfelt "Yes"!

Is there something you're currently doing that you actually want to say "No" to? If you can't articulate your "No" then you can't fully say yes to sex, can you? You're the only one who can really know what this would look like for you, but here are a few examples that might feel familiar:

- When I was married I often had sex with my husband because it put him in a better mood the next day. It seemed easier than the growing disquiet that settled in if we went too long without sex, by his definition of "too long."

- You know your partner loves sex in the morning but you always worry about morning breath or body odors. You want to freshen up first but it feels like you're breaking the mood. You know you're more likely to engage and enjoy the intimacy if you can brush your teeth first.

- Your boyfriend wants you to watch a sexy video with him before having sex. He thinks it will get you more excited. You're not sure about that so you hesitate. Maybe you should say yes once, sharing your reservations, but being open to how it might make you feel. You can always say "no thanks," even if you're in the middle of watching the video.

- "My husband doesn't understand that my dryness is partly due to not being fully aroused. He tends to rush straight into intercourse; I need more time to get ready. I might still want lube [and by the way—lube is a wonderful sex tool for all of us, dry or not] **and** I'd be more aroused and psychologically ready for sex if I could tell him that I want more of certain kinds of touch and kissing before intercourse."

- "Just once I want to tell my partner exactly what I want sex to be like. I want to describe in detail my ideal sexual experience. How he would undress me, where I want to be kissed, stroked, and how slowly I want it to happen. I don't always feel like the sex I'm having is the sex I'd like to be having."

- "I miss having sex but I don't know what to do and I don't want to find a partner just for sex. I feel a little awkward about self-pleasuring but don't I deserve to feel pleasure? Maybe I should try it out and see how it feels to be giving myself what I need."

If you could learn to speak about the things you want, to talk about what works and what doesn't, you would have better sex. You can begin to fully embrace and express your sexual needs, which has the effect of making you more receptive to, or excited about, having sex. Better sex in that you're not holding back, or feeling uncomfortable. Better sex because you're sharing the things that matter to you. Better sex because you found your voice and your partner listened and respected your needs. This is what consent, in this context, is all about.

You can't really enjoy an activity if you're not fully, truly consenting, or saying, "Yes!" You become an unwilling participant, possibly a bit resentful, or you tune out because you don't really want to be a part of what's happening. Could it be as simple as articulating your wants and desires? What would happen if you found a way to share your vision of intimacy? If you could express your thoughts and stop doing things just to please your partner?

Daily Exercise:

This is an exercise just for you. Be honest with yourself about this—write the answers down if you want, but take some time to really think about what happens when you're having sex with some degree of reluctance or ambivalence. Notice what it's doing to you emotionally and possibly physically.

- What are you doing during sex that you don't really want to do? Do you know why?
- What's your most frequent reason for not wanting sex?
- What do you want to change that would make you feel more excited about having sex?

- Are there things you want to say yes to, but something gets in the way? For example, you're angry with your partner so you deprive him. You're worried he won't like how you look, or that you won't please him in bed?
- Are there medical issues or physical concerns that affect your interest in having sex? Are you willing to talk about them?

WALKER THORNTON.

DAY 25

IT'S NOT ABOUT THE ORGASM

Please don't get so focused on orgasm that you forget to enjoy the journey. I've talked about sexual pleasure over the last few days' exercises. And you may have noticed that I have intentionally downplayed the subject of orgasms.

When our focus is "the orgasm" we try and we work and we hold our breath and we get all wrapped up in the "will I come?" game. Then when we don't have that orgasm we rate the whole experience as a failure. Our partner may feel let down as well or guilty they didn't do their job.

Admittedly, orgasms are wonderful. But there is much more to a fulfilling sexual experience than having an orgasm. When we take a walk, we enjoy the scenery. We stop to smell the flowers, to look at the sky, and we enjoy the whole journey.

Too often the pressure to be orgasmic in that "Big O" way derails the whole sexual experience for women. Start comparing your sex to movie sex or romance novels and it becomes more difficult to see your sexual experience as normal—however you define "normal" for you.

Whether solo or with a partner, engaging in sex should be a sensuous experience from start to finish. You want to play and explore, tease and pleasure. If your mind is focused on the orgasm you may miss out on 90% of the pleasure—and you may be reducing your chances of an orgasmic experience with such a narrow focus and even end up feeling anxious. That anxiety can easily become a "what if I can't have an orgasm next time?"

After playing with self-pleasuring (see Day 14) and trying out the sexual meditation exercise (see Day 20) you have gained a better understanding of your anatomy and what turns you on. You are feeling more alive and you are embracing your sexuality. This may help improve your ability to be more orgasmic, if you choose.

Daily Exercise:

- I want you to think about what you've learned so far in your sexual meditations and other times you may have engaged in self-pleasuring. What have you learned about your body? Are you feeling more pleasure at being touched?

- If you've given yourself an orgasm, was it something you want more of? Do you want to share your discoveries with your partner and teach him how to bring you to orgasm?

Remember, you don't have to include a partner. It is perfectly acceptable to be happy with whatever level of pleasure you experience during sex, partnered or solo. You are not comparing yourself to others; you're focusing on your own desire and what you want in your life.

DAY 26

REDEFINING SEX AS WE AGE

We hear it every day. Old people don't have sex.

I've heard a few women in their 50s say that they see no need for sex at their age. "I'm done with that and I don't miss it at all." As I discussed in Day 12, there are physiological benefits to remaining sexually active.

We are born sexual beings. Have you ever seen your young daughter or niece touch her genitals? They know the simple truth—it feels good. That pleasurable feeling never goes away, regardless of how old we are. Those of us with female genitalia possess a sex organ, the clitoris, whose sole purpose is to provide pleasure. With over 8000 nerve endings the clitoris is the general path to pleasure, if not orgasm, for most women. (See Figures)

The clitoris doesn't disappear. It doesn't shrivel up or fail to provide pleasure when we reach a certain age. The strength of our response to stimulation may change, but it is rare to find that our pleasure sensors shut down completely. Neither does our sense of pleasure at being touched, hugged, or kissed. We may not enjoy certain sexual acts at various points in our life but that's not a reason to give up all intimate touch.

If intercourse becomes challenging or painful, women often give up all forms of sex. They shut down and they close off that part of their life. One reason may be that we think of intercourse as the only path to sexual pleasure. I often talk to older adults about redefining sex as a way of expanding their options when intercourse is no longer comfortable or possible.

- Kissing, hugging, and cuddling provide pleasurable sensations and vital connections to a loved one. You can still experience sexual pleasure and feel connected to your partner from these intimate activities.
- Mutual masturbation can become an intimate act if you are willing to experiment openly with each other. You can kiss and touch each other while you pleasure yourselves.
- Oral sex is ideal if you find that vaginal intercourse has become painful post-menopause. Oral sex may also be pleasurable for your male partner because it can provide him orgasmic release if his erections become problematic. You can both practice giving as well as receiving.
- Fingers and toys, used alone or in conjunction, are wonderful ways to bring a woman to climax.

All of these acts fall into the category of "having sex" if you're willing to challenge the traditional definition of sex as the act of penetration, that is penis in vagina (referred to as PIV).

The question you should consider if you or a partner is reluctant to explore, is whether the intimacy is more important than the act of intercourse.

Daily Exercise:

Here are some questions for you to think about. You could write them in your journal or use them to start a conversation with your partner.

- What do you think about older people having sex? Do you think sex is important for adults of all ages?
- Is having sex important to you?
- If you're not having sex, why? Can you list the reasons? Was this your decision or your partner's? Do you feel that something is missing without some type of sexual intimacy in your life or relationship?
- What can you do to invite sexual pleasure into your life?

DAY 27

WAYS TO BUILD MUTUAL DESIRE

Dr. Patti Britton, a sexologist, says that most often when a couple is in her office to talking about their sex life, it's typically the male partner who is not interested in sex. *(1)*

I'm not going to address the topic of male desire here, but I am going to talk about ways to get both of you in the mood. Regardless of where your partner falls on the spectrum of sexual desire, unless he's completely uninterested (and then you might suggest he or the both of you seek professional help. See Endnotes for sex therapists) *(2)*, there are ways to ramp up the sense of anticipation and desire for both of you.

All sexual activity requires mutual desire. Giving and receiving requires that both partners want to engage in intimate activity. For all the reasons you may feel a loss of desire in your relationship, or as a single person, your partner will also have stressors and factors in his life that could affect his level of desire.

Let's suppose you want to have sex, what are you going to do to get both of you in the mood? Here are some ways you can engage your partner:

• Email, texting, and phone calls can be fun ways to spice things up. Hint at how excited you are about the date. Share a few details you know will excite him. Mention the sexy bra he loves, or a new red nail polish. Be as demure or racy as you want. Send a photo of you in your favorite lingerie. Be sure to send a preliminary text, "NSFW Picture coming" (NSFW is not safe for work). That way he's alerted and can say not now or be sure his cell phone is discreetly placed.

- Love notes. Hide a note in his briefcase or someplace he's likely to check while away. Write something racy and put it under his cup of coffee in the morning. Think about your current communication and use a message that ramps it up just a little. A sweet, *'you're wearing my favorite shirt today, love the way it looks on you'* might work, or it might be too sedate for what you have in mind. It's an individual thing.

- If feeling sensual is difficult for you—do something to get yourself all **"sexed up."** Do you have a fantasy that regularly pops up? If so, think about that as the evening approaches. Create your own fantasy—think about something your lover does to you and then embellish. This isn't about being faithful to the facts but rather to the spirit of an exciting image. Try reading a sexy story–do you have a favorite source for erotic writing? (See Day 3 for some ideas.)

- Arousal. In the hours leading up to your date, try a little self-pleasure. (See Day 14 for some hints.) Start the arousal process and it will help with your level of arousal later. That sexual energy will infuse you with a heightened sense that will carry through the evening. Tell him about it to get both of you excited and ready to go. You can give him a step-by-step report or wait until you're together to start the build-up of sexual tension.

Daily Exercise:

If you find yourself in the mood for intimacy, what can you do to communicate that to your partner and get him in the mood too?

- Is there something you wouldn't normally do that might get him excited? If you're home before he is could you meet him at the door in your/his favorite lingerie?
- Flirt with him during the evening. Be more attentive, touch his hand or get closer to him when you can. Do things you know he finds arousing. I remember being at a bar with a man I was seeing. I got up to go the bathroom and when I came back I discreetly opened my clenched hand to let him see that I was carrying my panties. Then I sat back down on the barstool next to him and pretended that everything was normal. The idea that I was sitting there in a dress, without my panties, drove him wild.
- Men like to know we want or desire them. They like being complimented on their sexual prowess. Try being direct and tell your partner that you crave his touch. Tell him you want to feel his lips on the nape of your neck. Or, that you "can't forget the way you make me feel the last time we were in bed, my legs wrapped around you...."
- Be the one to lead. If it feels right, tell him you want to touch him. You want sex—be explicit if you want or just ask permission to lead him to the bedroom and show him.

DAY 28

HANDLING DISAPPOINTMENT

In life things rarely happen as we envision them. Sometimes they just don't turn out the way we want them to, and that can happen with your quest to invite desire into your life. Nothing's guaranteed and I can't, as much as I would like to, promise that everything you read in this book will work for you. I do want to recognize your dedication and desire to embrace your sexuality. You're taking a big step; changes will continue to pop up as you discover more about yourself.

Not long ago I went through a period of not being able to orgasm with my partner. We know how to please each other and that knowledge has grown and made for some lovely intense times over the years. Suddenly I found myself unable to reach orgasm. Not just once, but several times in succession. We were doing the things that worked in the past. Needless to say it was disappointing for me; for him as well, I'm sure. I couldn't necessarily pinpoint one thing that might have pulled me off course. We couldn't pinpoint what might have caused this hiccup. And that's not unusual.

It happens to all of us at times—the cake doesn't rise;

our running time slows a little. The pleasurable feeling slips away right as we're ready to peak. Was I thinking about something else? Did I feel a shift in rhythm? Did I wait too long? Did we move differently? What happened?

For me it was about the orgasm; your personal experience might be about something else. Disappointment or finding an experience didn't live up to our hopes and expectations happens to all of us. The first thing to do is not let it mushroom into a bigger problem. Worrying about it can backfire if you get skittish the next time, like I did.

You can expect to encounter roadblocks on this journey to inviting desire into your life. What works one day may not bring the same respond the next time. Learning to have orgasms won't change a partner who doesn't give you the time and respect you deserve. New lingerie may make you feel like a million bucks but it won't guarantee a really romantic evening.

By inviting desire into your life you are seeking to change more than just your sex life. Awakening your body and shifting thought patterns will lead to changes in other areas. You've changed the dynamics of your relationship, if you're in a long-term relationship, and that will probably shake your partner up a little. Every change in life involves other minor adjustments—some we can see and anticipate, others are a complete surprise. This is not necessarily a bad thing; it's just a "different" thing.

As you take this journey, have compassion on yourself and those around you. Understand that, in daring to seek what you want, you will encounter obstacles. That's OK. Take it slow, be kind to yourself, engage in plenty of self-care and continue to invite in new ways to approach your body, intimacy, and relationships.

Daily Exercise:

- I'd like you to do a personal inventory. Get out your journal and write down what has changed since you started reading this book. Are you eating differently, sleeping more soundly? Are your taste buds more alive? Are there physical changes, emotional changes? Has your approach to sex changed? Are you finding yourself saying No to things that don't please you? Are you saying Yes to things you didn't before?

What's Different?

Are you experiencing challenges? If so, what can you do to address them? If your partner is also experiencing challenges can you schedule some time together in a non-intimate setting? A drive in the country, a walk in the park, or a long talk over coffee? It may be that he worries about being left behind. Ask him what his concerns are and discuss how the two of you can address them. Change can be hard for people. All you can do is acknowledge the changes and help a concerned partner see that this is about you, and him, and how you can enjoy each other.

DAY 29

PLANNING FOR PLEASURE

Before we end this journey of sexual discovery together I want to talk about the next steps. It's one thing to read about changes and even to journal your thoughts or practice the suggestions—but how will you continue your journey when our time together is over?

I encourage you to return to the book often and do the exercises again. You will probably have new ideas and levels of discovery, building on what you've already learned and implemented. But let's go further.

I want you to develop a plan to continually invite desire into your life in much the same way that you might plan a weekend trip or a day of errands. It's so important to make time for yourself, to create the opportunity to do things that give you pleasure. When lives get busy we tend to eliminate those little "extras" thinking they're not all that important. But they are. You are.

Daily Exercise:

- I invite you to create ideas, lists, plan dates, and anything that excites you to keep your thoughts focused on your pleasure and your desire. You don't need to set specific dates but the more detailed you are the more likely you are to implement your plan. It's not enough to just write out a goal, you want to create the steps leading to the goal to ensure success. For example:

My goal is to: Have one date night a month with my partner.
    Steps:
1. Talk to my partner and get agreement on the date night idea.
2. Get out our calendars and schedule the first date.
3. A few days before our date, talk about where we want to go, and what we want to. *Remember to be specific—vagueness can get in the way of accomplishing what you want.*
4. Be specific with my partner about the date—will there be sex? Dinner? What other things does he want to do on date night? What am I hoping for, or expecting?

Or maybe your goal is to think about the new life you want to live as a woman who embraces desire and pleasure? What steps would that include?

Don't let the idea of lots of details get in the way of creating a plan, but do remember that you need some concrete ideas of how to move forward.

There are other kinds of activities you might want to include in your desire plan. Remember that this is about **your** pleasure, so you add things just for you. Here are a few suggestions:

- Watch a sexy movie
- Get a massage
- Buy some new lingerie.
- Take an online course about some aspect of sexuality you want to learn more about. It could be erotic massage, learning to communicate in the bedroom, or learning a new technique.
- Plan a boudoir photo shoot.
- Visit your local sex toy shop.
- Go out with a friend for a night of fun. Go to an art opening, the movies, or other local event. Wear something that makes you feel good. Flirt, dance, watch, or whatever makes you feel alive and in touch with your body.
- Schedule alone time with your partner—it doesn't necessarily have to be of a sexual nature.
- Check-in with your partner. Talk about how you feel about your sex life. What do you each like about your current situation? What would you like add? Make plans.
- Revisit the Vision Board, collage, Pinterest page I talked about at the beginning of the book. Expand on what you've done, think about new things to add, new fantasies or ideas for what you want to do. Have fun playing with the possibilities.

Make your own list and save it in your journal. When you've got some time, refer to the list and try something fun. It doesn't necessarily need to be about sex; the goal is to indulge in things that bring you pleasure. It might be buying new flowers or having an erotic massage—it's up to you. Ask your partner for his suggestions if you want to include couples activities.

DAY 30

FINAL THOUGHTS

To invite desire into your life and explore your relationship with sexuality is a lifelong journey. We are sexual creatures from the moment we discover the pleasure of touch as a young child to the end of our lives.

Our desires and cravings don't end when we hit menopause or old age. They change. They may surge or they may become less vigorous but they don't have to disappear. We don't find a final answer—we keep growing and expanding as our wants and circumstances change.

Life will always be full of questions. We can't answer them all. Stepping into the unknown can be frightening and create self-doubt. What we can do is embrace the moment.

I hope this book has given you opportunities to embrace your sexuality. To embrace the woman you are now, at whatever age. To view your body and your sexual desire as natural and ripe with potential.

You have choices. And though we didn't specifically talk about choices, each step of the way--as you examine your sexuality and what you want out of life—you get to make a choice. Only you can decide what to embrace and what to let go of.

These are my hopes for you, that you will:

- Embrace the sexual you.
- Experience your life as a sexual journey.
- Step out of that self-limiting box.
- Learn to inhabit your body reverently and appreciatively.
- Find immense pleasure in living the life you've chosen for yourself.

We've spent a full month or more, looking at all the paths to getting in touch with your body and mind, in all things sexual. From becoming attuned to your senses to learning your body's orgasmic response and how to communicate your most intimate needs to a partner. You have a repertoire of activities, conversation starters, primers on sex toys and books to help you along with this journey.

Depending on your original starting point you may not be ready for all I've suggested. Remember, every journey starts with the first step.

I urge you to play with your sex life, to get sassy with your partner, or give yourself permission to play solo. Embrace who you are in this and every moment.

And thank you for the work you've done in committing to your own sexual needs.

ENDNOTES

1. Judith Plaskow, now retired from teaching at Manhattan College, is the co-editor of the Journal of Feminist Studies in Religion. The quote is from her book, *Standing Again at Sinai: Judaism from a Feminist Perspective.* New York: HarperOne; Reprint edition. 1991.

DAY 1 TOUCH

1. Ackerman, Diane. *A Natural History of Love.* New York: Random House, 2011.

DAY 3 WORDS

Permission granted for use of Neruda's poem by Exile Editions, Canada, and translator Gustavo Escobedo. 100 Love Sonnets can be found here: https://www.amazon.com/100-Love-Sonnets-Spanish%C2%96English-Bilingual/dp/1550963872/ref=sr_1_1

1. Neruda, Pablo. *100 Love Sonnets.* — Neruda was a Chilean poet and winner of the 1971 Nobel Prize for literature. Neruda is widely thought of as "a frank, sensuous spokesman for love." – Robert Clemens (in the Saturday Review) http://www.poetryfoundation.org/bio/pablo-neruda

2. Lawrence, D.H. *Lady's Chatterley's Lover.* — Written in

1928, this novel was widely censored. In 1960 its publication in the United States resulted in obscenity charges against publisher, Penguin Books. Lady Chatterley's Lover. Wikipedia. https://en.wikipedia.org/wiki/Lady_Chatterley's_Lover

3. Friday, Nancy. *My Secret Garden.* — First published in 1973, My Secret Garden ignited a firestorm of reactions across the nation—from outrage to enthusiastic support. In its time, this book shattered taboos and opened up a conversation about the landscape of feminine desire in a way that was unprecedented. - Wikipedia. https://en.wikipedia.org/wiki/My_Secret_Garden

4. Francoeur, Rae Padilla. *Free Fall, A Late-in Life Love Affair.* — "Francoeur succumbs entirely to the intensely physical and stimulating relationship she finds with this new man—allowing her body and mind to truly embrace pleasure and sexual desire—and shares intimate details of a love affair that changes everything, leading her to celebrate her sexuality and rediscover herself." Amazon. http://www.amazon.com/Free-Fall-Late---Life-Affair-ebook/dp/B003P9XC80/ref=sr_1_1

5. The writings of Anais Nin. "Nin is hailed by many critics as one of the finest writers of female erotica. She was one of the first women known to explore fully the realm of erotic writing, and certainly the first prominent woman in the modern West known to write erotica." https://en.wikipedia.org/wiki/Ana%C3%AFs_Nin

DAY 5 SELF-AFFIRMATION

1. George Sand is the pseudonym of Amantine-Lucile-Aurore Dupin, French novelist and memoirist.

DAY 9 OWNING YOUR SEXUALITY

1. Bergner, Daniel. *What Do Women Want?: Adventures in the Science of Female Desire*. HarperCollins Books. New York. 2013.

DAY 10 YOU *CAN* BE SEXUAL AND SINGLE

1. Komisaruk, Barry R., Beyer-Flores, Carlos, and Whipple, Beverly. *The Science of Orgasm*. Baltimore. Johns Hopkins University Press. 2006

Vaginal Atrophy As quoted in Day 17: The North American Menopause Society explains the loss of lubrication, "During perimenopause, less estrogen may cause the tissues of the vulva and the lining of the vagina to become thinner, drier, and less elastic or flexible—a condition known as *'vulvovaginal atrophy.'* Vaginal secretions are reduced, resulting in decreased lubrication."

DAY 11 HOW WE THINK ABOUT OUR SEXUALITY

1. Iyanla Vanzant: How to Rewrite Your Own Story. http://www.huffingtonpost.com/2013/01/02/iyanla-vanzant-how-to-rewrite_n_2371928.html

DAY 12 YOUR SEXUAL HEALTH

1. Galinsky AM, Waite LJ. Sexual Activity and Psychological Health As Mediators of the Relationship Between Physical Health and Marital Quality *The Journals of Gerontology: Series b.* online January 27, 2014 http://psychsocgerontology.oxfordjournals.org/content/

early/2014/01/24/geronb.gbt165.abstract

2. Fletcher, B. Have SEX to ward off dementia – especially if you're an 'older man' scientists claim. *Express.* Feb 16, 2016. http://www.express.co.uk/life-style/health/644291/having-sex-wards-off-dementia-especially-youre-older-man-scientists-claim.

DAY 13 WHAT IS AN ORGASM

1. Sexual Pleasure and Desire. The Kinsey Institute at Indiana University. http://kinseyconfidential.org/resources/sexual-pleasure-orgasm/#sthash.OERD6Da5.dpuf

2. Bahadur, N. Cosmo's Female Orgasm Survey Tells You Everything You Need To Know. HuffPost Women. March 23, 2015. http://www.huffingtonpost.com/2015/03/23/cosmo-orgasm-survey_n_6923934.html

DAY 17 LUBRICANTS

1. Changes in the Vagina and Vulva. The North American Menopause Society. http://www.menopause.org/for-women/sexual-health-menopause-online/changes-at-midlife/changes-in-the-vagina-and-vulva

2. Betty Dodson and Carlin Ross's article on lubricants. http://dodsonandross.com/blogs/carlin-ross/2012/05/our-favorite-lubricants

DAY 18 SEX TOYS

1. Betty Dodson is a PhD sexologist who has been one of the principal voices for women's sexual pleasure and health for over three decades. Paraphrased from http://dodsonandross.com/about-us

2. Good Vibrations is a sex toy shop in California with a good reputation and excellent resource articles. http://www.goodvibes.com/content.jhtml?id=how-to-choose-a-vibrator

3. Phthalates have been designated as "possible human carcinogens" by the United States Environmental Protection Agency (EPA) and are banned in many countries.

Note: The sex toy industry is essentially unregulated so you cannot expect to find the same level of safety standards, particularly in the cheaper toys. The softer and squishier a sex toy, the greater the chances it has been made with phthalates. http://kinseyconfidential.org/safety-dance-sex-toy-safety-generation/

Additional on-line resources for sex toys:

- Babeland.com
- Jimmyjane.com
- Lovecrave.com
- We-vibe.com

DAY 20 A SEXUAL MEDITATION

1. Joseph Kramer, Ph.D. founded the Body Electric School in Oakland, California in 1984, where he trained thousands

of professional massage therapists, erotic bodyworkers, and somatic educators. www.sexologicalbodywork.com

DAY 21 CREATING THE RIGHT ENVIRONMENT FOR SEX

1. The Liberator: a source for pillow wedges: https://www.liberator.com .

DAY 22 LEARNING TO ASK FOR WHAT YOU WANT

1. Betty Dodson—See Day 18

DAY 23 WHAT IF YOU'RE NO LONGER HAVING SEX?

1. Reid Mihalko is a sex and relationship expert, known as the Sex Geek, who teaches adults how to create more self-esteem, self-confidence, greater health, and satisfaction in and out of the bedroom. His website is: http://reidaboutsex.com/about-reid/

Books on Relationships:

Michaels, Mark A. & Johnson, Patricia. *Partners in Passion: A Guide to Great Sex, Emotional Intimacy and Long-Term Love.* California: Seal Press, 2014.

Nelson, Tammy. *Getting the Sex You Want: Shed Your Inhibitions and Reach New Heights of Passion Together.* Massachusetts: Quiver, 2008.

Perel, E. *Mating in Captivity: Unlocking Erotic Intelligence.* New York: Harper, 2007

Richo, David. *How to Be An Adult in Relationships: The Five Keys to Mindful Loving*. Massachusetts, Shambala Publications. 2002.

Schnarch, David, PhD. Passionate Marriage: Sex, Love, and *Intimacy in Emotionally Committed Relationships*. New York: Holt, 1998

DAY 27 WAYS TO BUILD MUTUAL DESIRE

1. Dr. Patti Britton is a Clinical Sexologist and Sexuality Educator. Patti, along with her partner Robert Dunlap, was one of the first professionals to develop a program for training sex coaches. http://drpattibritton.com/

2. AASECT—https://www.aasect.org/referral-directory This link allows you to search for the closest therapists.

FIGURES

Figure 1. Clitoris. Drawn by Amphis., Public Domain, Wikipedia

Figure 2. Anatomy of the Vulva. Cancer Research UK/Wikipedia Commons

FIGURES

FIGURE 1

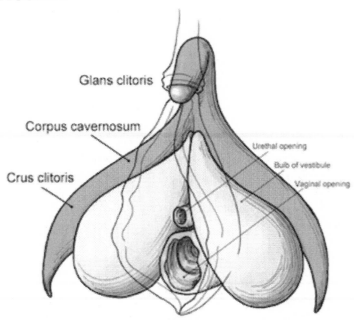

Glans clitoris

Corpus cavernosum

Crus clitoris

Urethal opening

Bulb of vestibule

Vaginal opening

FIGURE 2

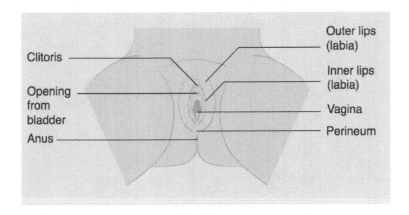

Clitoris

Opening from bladder

Anus

Outer lips (labia)

Inner lips (labia)

Vagina

Perineum

INDEX

ABOUT THE AUTHOR

Walker Thornton is a sex educator, speaker, and sexual health writer. A former executive director of sexual assault crisis centers, in Alabama and Virginia, with many years of nonprofit board experience at the local and state level, Walker now works to educate and support older women with sexuality-related issues.

Walker offers straight-talk about sex, occasionally mixing in personal stories to emphasize her point. Her mission is to help women embrace their sexuality in a way that feels comfortable at each stage of life. Her writing has appeared on the American Sexual Health Association website, Huffington Post, Better After 50, Senior Planet, and other sites. She is the Sexual Health Columnist for Midlife Boulevard and writes about midlife sexuality at Kinkly.com. Walker currently serves on the Sexuality and Aging Consortium of Widener University's Leadership Committee. She has presented at the Sexuality and Aging Symposium, CatalystCon, and in other venues across the country.

Walker lives in Charlottesville, VA, where she graduated from the University of Virginia in the early 70s. She has a Masters in Educational Psychology from the University of Georgia, and post-graduate work at North Carolina State University.

Made in the USA
Middletown, DE
04 January 2020

82575223R00092